DREAMS OF ANNE FRANK
ON MARGATE SANDS
CALL IN THE NIGHT

Bernard Kops

DREAMS OF ANNE FRANK
ON MARGATE SANDS
CALL IN THE NIGHT

OBERON BOOKS
LONDON

First published in this collection in 2000 by Oberon Books Ltd.
(incorporating Absolute Classics)
521 Caledonian Road, London N7 9RH
Tel: 020 7607 3637 / Fax: 020 7607 3629
e-mail: oberon.books@btinternet.com

Dreams of Anne Frank published by Samuel French Ltd in 1993
Dreams of Anne Frank published by Methuen in 1997

A catalogue record for this book is available from the British
Library.

ISBN 1 84002 132 2

Cover design: Andrzej Klimowski

Typography: Richard Doust

Author photograph: Matthew Thomas

Printed in Great Britain by Antony Rowe Ltd, Reading.

Contents

For Erica

FRESH AS NEW PAINT

Michael Kustow

The Jewish romance with theatre…

Before the First World War, Franz Kafka is swept away from his struggle with his father, his punctilious work in an insurance firm and his spidery subjectivity by the arrival in Prague of the Yiddish actors. In his diary he records his excitement at their vitality, their rough energy, their chutzpah. And also the desire he feels for the leading ladies, especially a Mrs Tschissik. No ingenue she, but a mature buxom woman who has lived and undergone passions for which Kafka still thirsts. He idolises her. A flirtation begins, across café tables after performances. He timidly offers a bouquet. Each night the Yiddish theatre plays a different melodrama, with bold emotions, big situations, central European folk morality, a fervour akin to Hassidism, the ecstatic singing and dancing religion of the shtetl Jews.

The last performance comes. Nothing has been consummated between Kafka and Mrs Tschissik. But Kafka has found a model for a greater robustness. He runs to the railway station as the troupe departs, races along the platform brandishing another bouquet for Mrs Tschissik. But the train leaves and the flowers wilt and his transient gaiety dims. Next day's diary entry records his 'intolerable loneliness'.

Bernard Kops, another Jew besotted with theatre, caught the theatre train. Early on, he joined the ever-travelling players. Theatre's gaiety and madness whip him around like a top. Volatile, passionate, lyrical, he was made for theatre, and the candid and dizzying pretences of theatre were made for his mercurial spirit. These three plays are the harvest of a lifetime under its spell.

They are also reflections of three aspects of his life. *Call in the Night* is a plunge into Nazism, a return to Berlin, an engagement with Germany, a homage to music. *On Margate Sands* comes from the jangling aftermath of the madness Bernard has experienced himself. *Dreams of Anne Frank*, a play for young people, not only comes from Kops the father, Kops the family man; it also draws its power and pain from its location. Anne Frank's Amsterdam was where his parents came from, where his father wanted to return in 1939, because he thought it would be safer for the Jews than London. But he was too poor to raise the fare. Bernard and his parents survived in Whitechapel; most of his Dutch family did not.

Disaster and disturbance shadow all these plays, all of Bernard's theatre. But they would not be theatre if they were not also joyful, if they did not sing and turn somersaults, if they did not have a sovereign disrespect for heavy reality. This is the root of their anguished poetry, their music-hall humour in the chamber of horrors. Bernard's virtuosity is especially apparent in *Call in the Night*, with its Chinese box structure, its wardrobe becoming a cabinet of transformations, its splitting of character between actors.

Here you feel the basis of Kopsian theatre. A restless fluidity, tossing and turning in the nightmare of what Auden called 'Europe's disgrace'. A kaleidoscope of fragmentary scenes and voices, a phantasmagoria. I think of the troubled European painters of this century when I read this play. The Belgian James Ensor, and his bruised carnival maskers. Max Beckmann driven from Germany, and his exiled kings and exhausted partygoers. The illuminated wartime picture-novel of Charlotte Salomon, who called it Life? Or Theatre? She, like Anne Frank, like the Kops family, was Dutch, and another Jewish artist inspired by theatre. The only train she caught was from Westerbork to Auschwitz.

On Margate Sands is about the emergence from a mental breakdown, and about the institutions that contain, in every sense, the mad. This play is propelled by an unnerving, raw hurdy-gurdy music, the discordance of the broken mind seeking to patch itself up again. Setting it in Margate, already a site in literary topography since T. S. Eliot, himself near breakdown, could 'connect nothing with nothing' on its beach, this play mines a vein of English provincial heartbreak. The sadness of unseasonal seaside resorts. The desolation of rooming houses, commandeered as asylums. And over everything, the funfair swings and roundabouts and fairy-lights and roller coaster of Margate's Dreamland, captured in Lindsay Anderson's early documentary, which moved Bernard.

There is always a dream and a dream-land, even in Bernard's most derelict landscapes. The popular songs that weave in and out of the drama, long before *The Singing Detective.* And the hero's dream of a paradise, in the shape of summers spent picking hops in Kent to make beer. There is always dream and life-force in the shape and lift of Bernard's lines, their poetry rooted in blunt, everyday, no-nonsense speech. It is the open-hearted truth-telling of the holy fool that Bernard knows himself to be. He just can't help blurting out the truth, sarcastic, vulnerable or extremely loving as it happens to be at that moment.

There is a tremendous sense of the present moment in these wind-whipped plays. And the present moment, the here and now, is theatre's vital ingredient. In these plays, Bernard Kops is so much the master of his art that he conjures, seemingly without effort, fierce transitions, transitory pageants, abrupt conjunctions and gear-changes to break open our diminished sense of reality. He is like that other theatre-obsessed Jew Marc Chagall. Not because of the superficial similarity of their dream landscapes, their defiance of gravity. But because of the story Chagall tells about his time with the Moscow Jewish State Theatre. They too were playing a folk play of Jewish life in the Russian *Pale of Settlement.* Chagall, who had designed and painted the scenery, full of marks and textures beyond realism, was standing in the wings behind an actor, who was dressed as a rabbi and due to go on. Chagall was unhappy with the actor's costume. As the entrance cue was approaching, he seized a paintbrush, transformed the actor's coat into a tapestry of many colours, and sent him spinning on stage.

These plays are as fresh, as immediate, as impulsive, as on-the-edge and urgent, as Chagall's brush.

Michael Kustow
London 2000

DREAMS OF ANNE FRANK

Characters

OTTO FRANK

ANNE FRANK

EDITH FRANK

MARGOT FRANK

MRS VAN DAAN

MR VAN DAAN

PETER VAN DAAN

MR DUSSEL

Dreams of Anne Frank was first produced at the Polka Theatre, London, on 3 October 1992, with the following cast:

OTTO FRANK, Edward Halstead

ANNE FRANK, Elizabeth Chadwick

EDITH FRANK, Kitty Alvarez

MARGOT FRANK, Celia Browning

MRS VAN DAAN, Hollie Garrett

MR VAN DAAN, Joe Cushley

PETER VAN DAAN, Tim Matthews

MR DUSSEL, Brett Fancy

Director, Leona Heimfeld

Designer, Fran Cooper

Music, David Burman

Setting: there is minimal scenery. Each scene is created by specific suggested images: there, but almost intangible, as if they might float away any moment (sometimes they do). This is to convey the fragility of the world around the players: a transient, temporary place they are just passing through. This is also to convey the fluidity of action, the dreams and imaginings of a young girl. The stage is uncluttered except for a triangular pile of clothes, downstage, off-centre with Anne's diary on top of the pile. There is also an upturned chair. Another important feature of furniture on this sparse stage is a typical 1930s radiogram set. Apart from its usual function of being a conduit for the outside world (news bulletins and miscellaneous music programmes), it will also play gramophone records, the source of the music that accompanies the songs in the play.
After the establishment of the set there is darkness.

ACT ONE

Arrival

Scene 1

A man enters. His clothes are formal. He is well dressed, spic-and-span, almost out of keeping with the scene he has entered. This is OTTO. He lifts the diary from on top of the pile of clothes, and speaks quietly without undue emotion.

OTTO: I'm Otto Frank. Anne Frank was my daughter, and she was very special. I survived the war. Somehow. Anne didn't. Survival was random. Pure chance. That morning when our liberators arrived, I just sat there. Numb. The gates were open but I had no spirit to get up and run. I knew then that my wife was dead and my neighbours. And my children were God knows where. I was breathing, yet I was dead. We were all dead, those departed and those still there on that morning. The gates were open and everything was incredibly silent and peaceful. All the guards had disappeared; as if they had been spirited away in the night, and that morning for the first time in ages I heard a bird singing. I think it was a blackbird because its song was so beautiful. It couldn't have been a nightingale. They avoided the skies above Auschwitz. Then we heard the sound of guns and great armoured vehicles on the move. Getting closer. Russian soldiers appeared. With chocolate and cigarettes, liniment and bandages. We didn't cheer. We just sat there, slumped and staring. Nobody spoke. The sun was so bright and the heat soaked into my bones. And then one soldier started to play his accordion. Suddenly someone danced. In slow motion. Others joined in. More and more. Dancing. Dancing. Soon, everyone who could stand on two legs was dancing. And laughing. And crying. I watched. I just watched. I loved my daughters. Margot and Anne. That goes without saying. But Anne was special. She didn't survive the war. But her words, her story, her secrets, her dreams are all here. In this book. The diary of Anne Frank. (*He opens the diary.*)

Scene 2

There has been a cross-fade, merging into this scene where ANNE appears. She enters, holding up a yellow star.

ANNE: Morning star. Evening star. Yellow star. Amsterdam, 1942. The German army occupies Holland. They have applied terrible rules that we must obey. Rules for Jews. That applies to me. 'Jews must wear a yellow star. Jews cannot go on trains. Jews must not drive. Jews cannot go shopping, except between three and five. Jews must only patronise Jewish shops.' We cannot go to the cinema, play tennis, go swimming. I cannot even go to the theatre. And now for the most frightening thing of all. They are beginning to round Jews up and take us away. Away from our homes, our beloved Amsterdam. A few days ago I celebrated my thirteenth birthday. My parents gave me this diary. It is my most precious possession. Yesterday I was just an ordinary girl living in Amsterdam. Today I am forced to wear this by our Nazi conquerors. Morning star. Evening star. Yellow star.

Scene 3

In their house OTTO, EDITH and MARGOT are celebrating their Sabbath. The candles are alight.

ANNE: It's the third of July, 1942. Mother's making Havdala. Sabbath's over.

EDITH: (*Sings 'Eliyahu Hanavi.' OTTO, MARGOT and ANNE join in the song.*) 'We look forward to the coming of the Messiah and world peace.'

ANNE: Amen! Margot! We can play.
(*The tablecloth and candles go.*)

ANNE: Hide and seek!

MARGOT: Find me, Anne! Find me! You can't find me!
(*ANNE covers her eyes with her fingers. MARGOT darts around and hides.*)

ANNE: (*Finding MARGOT.*) Gotcha!

MARGOT: You cheated. You looked. Cheat! Cheat!

ANNE: Liar! Liar! My turn. My turn.
(*They continue playing and laughing. ANNE hides.*)

ANNE: My parents were folding sheets.
(*OTTO and EDITH start folding sheets.*)
It was Sunday. The fifth of July. The day after American Independence Day. My mother pretended she wasn't crying.

EDITH: Do you remember, Otto? One year ago today, exactly. We were boating on the River Amstel. Remember that beautiful picnic? The wine.
(*With the sheets OTTO and EDITH mime being on the boat.*)
And that boat floating through that golden day.

OTTO: Yes, my love. And we shall go boating again, next year.

ANNE: Then Father made the announcement. I remember his exact words.

OTTO: Listen, children. Please. I must tell you something. We're going into hiding.

ANNE: Hiding? Great! They're joining in our game. You hide, Mother, with Margot. We'll find you.
(*They laugh.*)

OTTO: Be sensible, Anne. You know what I mean. We've been preparing for this for a long time. And now that time has come.

EDITH: We must be strong. And brave.

ANNE: When are we going into hiding?

OTTO: Thursday.

ANNE: Hurray!

MARGOT: Hurray!
(*MARGOT and ANNE stand close, arms around each other.*)

ANNE: Where are we going to hide?

EDITH: You'll find out soon enough.

ANNE: I was asking Daddy!

MARGOT: Anne!

ANNE: Will we be alright?

EDITH: Of course, my love. We'll always be alright.

OTTO: There will be others hiding with us. The Van Daans.

ANNE: Who?

EDITH: You know the Van Daans. Their son Peter is about your age.

ANNE: I don't remember him.

MARGOT: I do.

ANNE: Come on, Margot. Let's finish our game.

EDITH: Girls. No time to waste. Playtime's over.

ANNE: What do I leave behind? What can I take?

OTTO: Only necessary things.

EDITH: Absolute essentials.

ANNE: (*Gets her satchel.*) Essentials. My school satchel. I'm going to cram it full. Hair curlers.

MARGOT: Really!

ANNE: Mind your own business, Margot! What are you taking?

MARGOT: Absolute essentials.

ANNE: Handkerchiefs. School books. Film star photographs. Joan Crawford. Bette Davis. Deanna Durbin. Mickey Rooney. Comb. Letters. Thousands of pencils. Elastic bands. My best book. *Emil and the Detectives.* Five pens. (*She smells a little bottle.*) Nice scent. Oh yes! Mustn't forget my new diary. Have you seen it? (*She has put all her things into her satchel but she has not included her diary.*) We're going into hiding. Going into hiding.
(*The others all are busy packing.*)
Four days later. It was Thursday the ninth of July. I shall never forget that morning. It was raining. Imagine leaving your house, maybe forever.

MARGOT: Anne. Please don't cry.

ANNE: I'm not! Liar! (*Crying.*) I'm laughing. (*Laughing.*)

MARGOT: You're mad.

ANNE: I must be mad to have you as a sister. Sorry, Margot. You're my favourite sister.

MARGOT: Silly. I'm your only sister.

ANNE: Everyone says you're beautiful and intelligent. And I'm the cheeky one. But I don't mind, really. I'm brilliant.

MARGOT: Exactly.

(*They laugh.*)

ANNE: I'm so happy. In hiding we no longer have to obey the Germans, the master race. No more dreaded rules for Jews.

OTTO: Girls!

(*Suddenly they are ready and all stand looking at the house.*)

ANNE: Goodbye, house.

HOUSE: (*EDITH's taped voice.*) So, you're leaving. How could you do this to me?

ANNE: Sorry. It wasn't us.

HOUSE: I know. I'll miss you all.

ANNE: We'll always remember you.

HOUSE: And I'll always hear you. I have your laughter, your singing, soaked in my walls, echoing forever.

(*We hear laughter and singing.*)

Goodbye, Frank family.

ANNE: House! Don't cry.

HOUSE: I'll try.

ANNE: Thank you for everything. My brain is at a fairground, on the rollercoaster. Up and down. Happy. Sad. Afraid. Excited. My emotions are racing. My imagination spilling over. After all, I am a creative artist. I'm going to be a writer when this war is over.

(*OTTO, EDITH and MARGOT wait as she lingers.*)

EDITH: Anne!

MARGOT: We're waiting.

ANNE: Imagine leaving your house, forever.

(*They are all about to go. But…*)

Diary! Can't go without my diary. (*She takes up the diary and opens it.*)

DIARY: Hello, Anne.

ANNE: Hello, Diary.

DIARY: Nothing entered in me yet. Your world is a fresh clean page.

ANNE: Marvellous.

DIARY: Anne! Remember, even if you are locked away, all is possible in your head.

ANNE: (*Taking up the diary's speech.*) 'You can be trapped in a box, or in sadness, but you can travel in your mind. You can be imprisoned in a basement or an attic, but you can go anywhere. In your dreams you are free, the past, the present, the future. It is all open to you within my pages. Use me well.' (*As herself.*) I promise. I shall write everything down. Everything. Thoughts. Events. Dreams.

DIARY: That's what I'm here for.

ANNE: I shall confide my secrets. Only to you.

DIARY: Whatever you write is safe with me. No one else will ever know. It's our secret.

ANNE: Yes. Forever. (*Clutching her diary close.*) Let's go.

MARGOT: What's that?

ANNE: My diary.

MARGOT: Why you holding it so close? Is it that precious?

ANNE: I couldn't survive without my diary.

EDITH: Come on.

(*OTTO, EDITH and MARGOT leave.*)

ANNE: (*Sings.*)

FATE GAVE ME A YELLOW STAR.

A BADGE TO TELL THEM WHO I AM.

I'M ANNE FROM AMSTERDAM.

ANNE FROM AMSTERDAM.

I'M ANNE FRANK AND I'M A JEW,

BUT I'M THE SAME AS YOU AND YOU.

OR YOU OR YOU AND YOU.

BUT THEY GAVE ME A YELLOW STAR.

YELLOW STAR.

THE STAR'S TO PUT ME IN MY PLACE,

TO WEAR IT AS A BADGE OF SHAME,

BUT I'M ANNE FROM AMSTERDAM.

I'M PROUD OF WHO I AM.

WE HAVE TO HIDE AWAY FROM LIGHT

BECAUSE THEY COME FOR US AT NIGHT.

AND PACK US OFF TO GOD KNOWS WHERE,

AND ALL WE HAVE IS WHERE WE ARE.

BUT FATE GAVE ME THE YELLOW STAR.

YELLOW STAR.

Scene 4

The Frank family arrive in the attic, carrying boxes, cases and blankets. First they explore the dimensions of their hiding place.

OTTO: This attic. Our secret hiding place.

MARGOT: It's very small.

ANNE: It's very large.

MARGOT: Anne! Your imagination! Come down to earth for once.

ANNE: (*At the window.*) Look down there. That's earth. It's not such a nice place to be at this moment. I'm sleeping up there! Right! Everything's settled. I feel so, so happy. Be happy. Please.

MARGOT: I'll try.

ANNE: Are you depressed?

MARGOT: I'm alright. When I do get depressed your spirit lifts me. But I do wish those other people would arrive. I believe the boy's name is Peter. How old is he?

ANNE: Who cares? What would you like to do more than anything else in the world?

MARGOT: Go ice skating.

ANNE: Listen! We are cooped up here and we can go nowhere. Therefore – we can go everywhere. In captivity you can be free inside your head. (*She orders up a scene.*) Ebony black mauve sky. Shivering silver moon. Frozen over vast expanse of lake. Shimmering, diamond sheet of ice. There! It's all yours.

MARGOT: Can I? Are you sure?

ANNE: Absolutely! If you really want to. Use your imagination and it's all yours. Go on! What are you waiting for?

(*MARGOT goes ice skating on the frozen lake.*)

MARGOT: It's wonderful! I'm skating. I'm skating. Join me! Join me!

(*ANNE joins her and soon they are both skating and laughing joyously. But then ANNE suddenly stops.*)

Spoilsport! What's wrong?

ANNE: Someone walked over my grave.

(*ANNE switches on the radio, twiddles the dial. A victory 'V'*
drumbeat is heard.)

ANNOUNCER: 'This is the BBC in London calling
Europe. We now present Carrol Gibbons and his dance
band from the Savoy Hotel. In the heart of London.
(*The music continues softly in the background. MARGOT*
and ANNE playfully dance together as they put things away.
They laugh.
There is a noise outside. The family freeze with fear.)

MARGOT: Are we betrayed?

OTTO: Leave it to me. (*Cautiously listens at the door.*)

Scene 5

OTTO opens the trapdoor. Outside we hear a woman laughing, raucously.

OTTO: It's alright. It's the Van Daans.
(*Much relief.*)

EDITH: Thank God. Now, don't forget, girls: let them settle
in. Don't intrude.
(*The Van Daans enter with their belongings. They try to be*
quiet but are very loud.)

VAN DAAN FAMILY: (*In unison.*) We're the Van Daans.

EDITH: Ah! The Van Daans!

MRS VAN DAAN: (*Booming voice. Laughing.*) I'm Mrs Van
Daan. We're so happy to be here. This is my husband.

MR VAN DAAN: How do you do?
(*Suddenly they are stiff and formal as they all shake hands.*)

FRANK FAMILY: How do you do?

MRS VAN DAAN: And this is my son. Peter.

FRANK FAMILY: How do you do?

ANNE: (*Gently mocking.*) How do you do? How do you do?

MR VAN DAAN: Yes. Thank God at last we're safe
and secure.

EDITH: What's it like outside?

MR VAN DAAN: Let us change the subject. Please.

MRS VAN DAAN: (*Ignoring the plea.*) It's terrible out there.
It breaks my heart.

MR VAN DAAN: The Germans are doing exactly what they promised. After all it's all there in *Mein Kampf* and the Nuremberg Laws.

MRS VAN DAAN: Since you went into hiding it's got much worse, I can tell you. Every day worse and worse. They're dragging people off the street, from their beds. I saw them on the other side of the road this morning, carrying an old man out.

MR VAN DAAN: Please. Can we change the subject?

MRS VAN DAAN: Mr Levene, ninety-two years old, too crippled to walk, they carried him out and threw him into a truck, like a sack of potatoes.

MARGOT: Where did they take him?

EDITH: God knows where. God rest his soul.

OTTO: Please. We must now concentrate on us. On how we all can live together in harmony.

MR VAN DAAN: Absolutely.

MRS VAN DAAN: (*Grabbing a chair and sitting down.*) I like this chair. It's perfect for my back.

ANNE: I'm sorry; that's my chair.

MR VAN DAAN: Your chair? Ha! Ha! Ha! That's funny.

ANNE: It's my chair! My chair! It's mine.

MRS VAN DAAN: I see. And does it have your name on it?

EDITH: Sarcasm is the lowest form of wit.

MARGOT: Exactly.

ANNE: I want my chair. Give it to me.

MRS VAN DAAN: It's mine. How dare you?

(*They struggle for the chair.*)

EDITH: Anne! Behave!

MRS VAN DAAN: Yes. Respect your elders.

ANNE: If you were respectable I would.

EDITH: Anne! I won't tell you again.

OTTO: Please! This is absurd.

MR VAN DAAN: Absolutely. How right you are, Mr Frank.

OTTO: We must behave reasonably. If we balance things out inside we may be able to survive when we finally go out. May we show you around?

MRS VAN DAAN: That would be very nice.

OTTO: I've got it all sorted. Come. Everything should work very well if we obey certain rules.

EDITH: And if we are all tolerant of each other and understanding.

MRS VAN DAAN: Hear! Hear!

MR VAN DAAN: You echo my sentiments entirely.
(*The four adults leave to look around the attic. The three young people remain and at first are silent and embarrassed.*)

MARGOT: Hello, Peter.

ANNE: Why are you saying hello? We've said hello already.

MARGOT: How old are you?

PETER: Why do you want to know?

MARGOT: No reason.

PETER: I'm fifteen. How old are you?

MARGOT: Why do you want to know?

PETER: No reason.

MARGOT: I'm sixteen.

EDITH: Margot! Would you come here please?

MARGOT: Yes, Mother. (*MARGOT joins the adults.*)

PETER: How old are you?

ANNE: Why do you want to know?

PETER: No reason.
(*The others return and start to unpack. MRS VAN DAAN drops an iron on the floor.*)

MR VAN DAAN: Clumsy wumsy.

OTTO: We must remember to be quiet. There are people right below us who don't even know we're here.

ANNE: Yes. We must have hush.

MARGOT: And shush.

PETER: Sneezing is not allowed. Excuse me. Atishoo.

ANNE: Hiccups are not allowed. (*Hiccups.*) 'Scuse me.

MARGOT: Nor snoring. (*Snores.*)

ANNE: Nor coughing.
(*All three snore.*)

PETER: Nor talking in your sleep.

MARGOT: Nor the belly grumbles.

ANNE: Nor heaving. Nor breathing. Nor crying. Nor dying.

EDITH: Anne!

MR VAN DAAN: Mr Frank, don't worry. It's nice they're getting on so well. And us.

EDITH: We have to. After all, this one little attic is our whole world, from now on. God help us.

MR VAN DAAN: He will. I told you I had a little chat with Him last night.

PETER: Dad!

MRS VAN DAAN: Isn't he funny? Isn't he lovely? (*She pinches MR VAN DAAN's cheek.*) Ooh! I could eat him.

MR VAN DAAN: Delicious! Delilah!

MRS VAN DAAN: Mr and Mrs Frank, I would just like you to know that you will find us totally cooperative. I couldn't wish to hide with nicer people.
(*She does not notice that ANNE is wickedly aping her words.*)
And you will find us equally nice and responsible. You will also find that I am a modest person. A modest, humble and quiet person. Humble and unassuming. Courteous. Gracious. Polite. Self-effacing. Nice. Decent. Pleasant. Gentle. Spic-and-span. Affable. And unpretentious. And harmless. Inoffensive. Well- mannered. Conciliatory. Sociable. Friendly. Civil. Dignified. Unimposing. Shy. Retiring. Reserved. Almost bashful. In other words I know my place and I never fuss.
(*She spins around and discovers ANNE mimicking her.*)
How dare you! How dare you!

EDITH: She's only a child. She didn't mean anything.

MRS VAN DAAN: If she was only my child I would scold her.

EDITH: Apologise.

ANNE: I'm sorry.

MRS VAN DAAN: You are a spoiled little brat. A monster.

EDITH: Please do not call my child a monster.

MRS VAN DAAN: I will if she behaves monstrously.

EDITH: You are an impossible woman.

MRS VAN DAAN: What? Me? I am the most possible person you could ever come across.

MR VAN DAAN: Let's all play cards. Yes? Wonderful!

(*OTTO and EDITH look pained. But she nods. They all sit down.*)

Rummy?

(*They play cards. MARGOT looks at PETER who looks at ANNE. ANNE goes to the window. There she sees light and dark. Light and dark.*)

ANNE: Days pass, nights pass. Nothing happens. That's life. Passing before your eyes. And if you write about it, record it, at least you have proof it was there. It's all in the words.

(*There is a sudden knocking on the door.*)

MARGOT: (*Rushes to EDITH.*) Are we betrayed?

(*Then silence for a long moment.*)

OTTO: Leave this to me. (*Goes to the door, listens.*)

Scene 6

OTTO opens the door and is handed a birthday cake.

OTTO: It's a gift from helping hands.

ANNE: Peter! Here's your cake.

PETER: Cake? Is it my birthday already?

MARGOT: Of course it's your birthday, silly. As if you didn't know.

MR VAN DAAN: Cake? How have I survived without cake?

ALL: (*Sing.*) 'Happy birthday to you – '

MR VAN DAAN: (*Starts cutting the cake.*) Here! Shove this in your cakehole, darling.

MARGOT: Peter! What can I get you for your birthday?

PETER: The Eiffel Tower.

MARGOT: Okay. I'll wrap it up tomorrow morning.

MRS VAN DAAN: How do we know we can trust those helping hands?

OTTO: They've proved themselves, these Dutch Christians.

MRS VAN DAAN: I trust no one.

OTTO: We have no choice. We are in their hands.

EDITH: If they're caught helping us it's certain death. They're very brave. I wonder whether I would do the same for them if they were in our position.

(*They all go silent.*)

ANNE: Do you like him?

MARGOT: Who?

ANNE: Peter.

MARGOT: Not much. A bit, maybe.

(*Sirens sound.*)

ANNE: They're bombing Amsterdam again. Look! Look at the sky! The tracery is so beautiful.

(*The sound of bombs falling.*)

OTTO: Anne! Come away from that window.

MRS VAN DAAN: Peter!

OTTO: Please!

EDITH: Anne! Margot! Come here, darling.

(*MARGOT goes to her mother.*)

MR VAN DAAN: Are you scared, blossom?

MRS VAN DAAN: You kidding? With my caveman beside me?

OTTO: The more the British bomb the better. I rejoice every time the RAF are overhead.

EDITH: As long as we all don't die in the process.

MR VAN DAAN: (*Sings to the tune of 'Coming Round the Mountain'.*) 'Oh we'll all go together when we go – '

ANNE: My beloved Amsterdam.

OTTO: (*Joining ANNE.*) Come bombs, give those Nazis hell.

(*Cuddles his daughter as bombs come closer and closer.*)

MRS VAN DAAN: We have to have faith, Mrs Frank.

EDITH: Yes. If only there was a shop where we could buy some.

MR VAN DAAN: Mr Frank! Let's get on with the game.

(*OTTO returns to the game. The all-clear sounds. Day and night and day outside.*)

ANNE: All clear! The best sound in the world. I long to hear it. Yet I want them beaten. Day after day after day the same. Playing cards. Sleeping. Getting up. Morning always brings breakfast. And fresh hope. It's morning, everyone!

ALL: Morning?

MRS VAN DAAN: Gosh! Time just flies. Life! Grab it while you can.

(*MR VAN DAAN grabs her. She laughs. They all leave their card game.*)

EDITH: Breakfast, everyone. Come and get it.

MR VAN DAAN: (*Impersonating Billy Cotton.*) 'Wakey!
Wakey!' Come and get it. (*He sings a couple of lines from
'Somebody stole my girl' then cuddles his giggling wife.*)

ANNE: I love early morning. Maybe today the war will be
over. If wishes could fly all my hopes would hold up the
sky. Miracles, like everything else, are in short supply
these days. Listen! I can hear the beautiful song of
a blackbird. And children, in a school playground. If
only I could be at school, playing with my friends. Will
I ever see them again?

MARGOT: What's the time?

ANNE: You mean, what is time? It's half past forever.
Twenty past never.

(*There is a sudden knock on the door.*)

ANNE: It's something nice again, I'm sure.

OTTO: Someone to tell us the war is over.

MRS VAN DAAN: A beautiful, shapely swimming costume.

EDITH: A new hat. Elegant. Stunning.

MR VAN DAAN: A joke book, chockablock with howlers.

MARGOT: Some knitting patterns.

PETER: Chocolate éclairs. A bowl of hot custard.

(*They all rush to the door just as OTTO opens it.*)

Scene 7

MR DUSSEL: (*Entering. He gives OTTO his card.*) Mr Dussel,
at your service. You have been expecting me.

OTTO: Yes, we were alerted that you would possibly be
joining us in our hiding place. I'm Otto Frank. This is
my wife and my two daughters.

(*They shake hands.*)

MRS VAN DAAN: How do you do? We haven't been
introduced.

MR DUSSEL: What nice, glistening teeth you have. I can
see they are all your own.

MR VAN DAAN: I didn't quite catch your name.

MR DUSSEL: (*Sings.*)

I'M DUSSEL THE DENTIST, SEEKER OUT OF CAVITIES.

NOT CARING FOR YOUR TEETH IS ONE OF LIFE'S DEPRAVITIES

KEEPING THEM CLEAN AND FREE OF GOO
IS THE ONLY THING THAT SHOULD MATTER TO YOU.
I'M DUSSEL THE DENTIST, SEEKER OUT OF CAVITIES.
NOT CARING FOR YOUR TEETH IS ONE OF LIFE'S DEPRAVITIES.
SO YOU CAN EXPECT ME EVERY MORNING, WITHOUT
WARNING, EVERY MORNING WITHOUT WARNING,
TO STAB AND TO POKE FOR BACTERIAL DECAY.
SO COME MY FRIENDS WITHOUT DELAY.
NO TIME TO BE LOST
JUST BEND TO MY WILL
I'LL SOLVE ALL YOUR PROBLEMS WITH MY PROBE AND
MY DRILL. PROBE AND DRILL! AND PROBE AND
DRILL AND PROBE AND DRILL. AND PROBE AND DRILL.
I'M DUSSEL THE DENTIST, SEEKER OUT OF CAVITIES.
NOT CARING FOR YOUR TEETH IS ONE OF LIFE'S DEPRAVITIES
KEEPING THEM CLEAN AND FREE OF GOO
IS THE ONLY THING THAT SHOULD MATTER TO YOU.

Right! Line up. Open wide!

(*All are petrified. They line themselves up like soldiers but PETER and MARGOT giggle.*)

SILENCE! This is not to be enjoyed. (*MR DUSSEL is about to probe into MRS VAN DAAN's mouth.*) Wait! Someone's missing! Someone is disobeying the rules.

MRS VAN DAAN: It's her over there. Saint Anne of Amsterdam.

MR DUSSEL: Why is she staring into space?

PETER: She's writing a book about the human race.

MR VAN DAAN: She thinks it makes her special.

MR DUSSEL: No one is exempt. Call her over here.

MARGOT: Leave her alone. She's just writing.

PETER: She's writing all this. Writing all us.

MRS VAN DAAN: She's never really with us.

MR DUSSEL: Well, I personally refuse to be written about. Where was I? Oh yes! You! (*He now probes deep into MRS VAN DAAN's mouth.*) Nasty! My God! Nasty! Nasty! (*MRS VAN DAAN lets out a piercing scream.*)

ANNE: (*Wickedly.*) Shuusshh! (*Laughs from her distance.*)

MRS VAN DAAN: Nasty girl! Come down to earth.

EDITH: What's it like out there?

OTTO: Darling.

MRS VAN DAAN: Look at his eyes. It's terrible. Tell us.

MR VAN DAAN: Precious! If the world's coming to an end, why broadcast it?

MRS VAN DAAN: Listen.

MR DUSSEL: It was the middle of the night. I heard a scream. I saw the family next door being dragged out. I thought it was a dream. It was all in slow motion. The baby cried. The mother tried to keep her quiet. The soldiers kept hitting, hitting with their guns. The child went silent. I couldn't look any more.

EDITH: Things have gone from bad to worse since we went into hiding.

PETER: We should have made a stand. We should have died fighting.

OTTO: What? Us? Against the whole German army?

MR DUSSEL: Incidentally, where do I sleep?

OTTO: Over there. Up, near Anne.

ANNE: Oh no!

MR DUSSEL: (*Muttering.*) I see. Still, could be worse. Plenty of mouths to work upon up here. We must surgery on. (*Unpacks his things.*)

ANNE: You see, Peter, time is a mystery. What has happened is happening again. What is about to happen has happened before. Sleep is the only thing that separates yesterday from tomorrow. Memory has no continuity. Thoughts, like a jigsaw, are all over the place.

PETER: I see. (*He doesn't.*)

MARGOT: I don't either.

MRS VAN DAAN: If I had daughters they would be helping.

MARGOT: (*Goes to the women.*) May I help you with dinner?

MRS VAN DAAN: What a good girl.

EDITH: Margot's an angel. Anne? Well – she's different.

MRS VAN DAAN: Of course. She's almost an adult. At least she's a dutiful daughter.

EDITH: Anne's also good. It's just that she gets carried away with her book of words.

MR VAN DAAN: Hmmmm! Something smells good. What's for supper, precious?

MRS VAN DAAN: Me.

MR VAN DAAN: Hmmm! Yummy. Yummy.

EDITH: It's amazing. It seems we've only just got up, yet it's evening already and we're about to have dinner. Time flies.

MRS VAN DAAN: Come and get it. Lovely grub.

PETER: Great. Starving.

MARGOT: What is it?

ANNE: What else. Potatoes and cabbage.

PETER: Boiled together, as usual.

ANNE: How did you guess?

EDITH: Dig in.

(*They all eat.*)

MRS VAN DAAN: Lovely to see a man with a healthy appetite.

MR VAN DAAN: You said it. What I wouldn't do for a nice slice of cow.

ANNE: Help yourself! Eat your wife! (*Pointing at MRS VAN DAAN who hasn't heard.*)

(*The others splutter and laugh.*)

EDITH: Anne!

MRS VAN DAAN: What did she say?

MR VAN DAAN: Nothing, sweetheart. You know I've been thinking. If God lived on earth we'd all break his windows.

MRS VAN DAAN: Listen, young lady. I know you said something nasty about me. You're rude and ill-mannered.

EDITH: Apologise!

ANNE: You have to dream to get away. Just think of it. Imagine being locked away, in an attic with seven others day after day. The noises they make, the games they play. You have to dream to get away. Just think of it. The way they sit, the way they smell, their rumbling tummies could make life hell. How I wish I could live in a shell. Just think of it. To get away, to get away, from these same old faces that get in the way. These people I'm trapped with day after day. You have to dream to get away. Or lose yourself in French verbs. (*Takes up an exercise book and writes in it. PETER hovers.*)

PETER: What are you doing now?

ANNE: Mustn't fall behind.
PETER: With what?
ANNE: Lessons.
PETER: What sort of lessons?
ANNE: French! If you really must know.
PETER: I speak French.
ANNE: Really? Say something.
PETER: *Je vous aime.*
   (*ANNE laughs.*)
   What's wrong?
ANNE: If you really loved someone you should say *Je t'aime.'*
PETER: You obviously know more than me. (*Nervous.*)
   I – I know! Why don't we do schoolwork together?
ANNE: No thank you.
PETER: Sorry. Excuse me for breathing. (*Retreats.*)
MR VAN DAAN: Once upon a time there was a man who
   told jokes all the time. (*Laughing already.*) Stop me if
   you've heard this –
   (*The children groan.*)
MARGOT: Please excuse me. (*Leaves the table.*)
PETER: Excuse me. (*Leaves the table.*)
   (*ANNE leaves the table and brushes MARGOT's hair. PETER
   watches them.*)
ANNE: I wish you wouldn't watch me all the time.
MARGOT: (*Quietly to herself.*) Wish someone would watch me.

Scene 8

ANNE goes to the radio and twiddles the knob. There is interference.

ANNOUNCER: This is the BBC Home service. Calling
   Europe. We bring you the Prime Minister of Great
   Britain. Mr Winston Churchill.
ANNE: Good evening, Mr Churchill.
CHURCHILL: Good evening, Anne. You sound troubled.
ANNE: It's just that I would like you to tell your Air Force
   to drop more bombs on Amsterdam. But tell them to
   take care to only bomb the Nazis and not our beautiful
   city or the Dutch people in their air-raid shelters or
   people like us, in hiding.

CHURCHILL: I'll do my best.

ANNE: Thank you.

CHURCHILL: I believe you are writing a diary, Anne?

ANNE: Yes, Mr Churchill.

CHURCHILL: Keep up the good work.

ANNE: I shall.

CHURCHILL: Take care of yourself and don't catch cold.

ANNE: Thank you, sir.

CHURCHILL: Not at all. And now I would like to say a few words to the others. Goodnight.

ANNE: Goodnight.

OTTO: Anne! Can you please stop talking to yourself.

ANNE: I was talking to Mr Churchill.

OTTO: Yes. Of course you were.

ANNE: He wants to say something to all of you.

ANNOUNCER: This is the BBC Home service. Calling Europe. We bring you the Prime Minister of Great Britain, Mr Winston Churchill.

OTTO: It is him.

(*They huddle around the radiogram.*)

CHURCHILL: This is not the end, not even the beginning of the end. But it is the end of the beginning.

(*An air-raid siren sounds and we hear the crump of bombs. The others seem suddenly dispirited.*)

ANNE: I wish this day was over.

(*It gradually gets dark.*)

Nightfall! Look! Suddenly you notice it.

(*They all start to make ready for bed.*)

And once again another deadly symphony begins.

(*Bombs whistle down. The place shakes. Everyone freezes with fear as the bombs come close.*)

But I also love nights. I watch them come and go. Again and again. Thankful that tomorrow will come sooner. And the end of the war. And freedom. Oh God, how long can we survive here?

CHURCHILL: Anne! Be brave. Be strong.

ANNE: Thank you, Mr Churchill.

Scene 9

MRS VAN DAAN: Bedtime already? Surely we only just
got up?

(*Everyone starts washing and gargling.*)

EDITH: You're right. There doesn't seem to be enough time
for anything.

MR VAN DAAN: But you've always got time for your
own funeral.

MRS VAN DAAN: Treasure? Why so morbid?

MR VAN DAAN: Sorry, poppet. I've always got time
for you.

OTTO: This is the end of the beginning.

EDITH: But surely it's the beginning of the end.

MRS VAN DAAN: No. The beginning of the middle of
the end.

MR DUSSEL: More like the middle of the beginning of
the end.

MRS VAN DAAN: This means it's the beginning of the
end! In that case the war's almost over. We're going to
survive.

OTTO: Listen! Everyone. You heard what Winston Churchill
said. It's only the end of the beginning.

EDITH: There's still a long way to go.

(*On radio Vera Lynn sings 'Silver Wings in the Moonlight'.*)

MARGOT: How will we be able to survive this?

EDITH: We are a nation of survivors. We crossed the desert.

MRS VAN DAAN: We should have stayed on the other side.

MR DUSSEL: We are Jews. We endure.

MARGOT: We are Dutch. Almost.

MR DUSSEL: We survived the wilderness. With all teeth
intact.

MARGOT: We will survive all this, won't we, Anne? Anne?
Tell me if you know.

ANNE: Don't worry. In my diary people and humanity and
good and justice will triumph over evil. In my diary I know
we are all safe and we shall all be saved.

MRS VAN DAAN: That diary is not the world.

ANNE: It is my world. (*Makes an entry into the diary.*)

OTTO: That diary might be our witness. Who knows? It could warn the world not to fall into the dark again.

MR DUSSEL: I want to survive. Here and now. Not in words.

MRS VAN DAAN: Damn the diary. I'm going to bed.

OTTO: Look at my daughter. She's dreaming again.

EDITH: Remember, Otto, all those years ago? Before we had kids. And we went on holiday to Berlin.

OTTO: I remember.

EDITH: And all the leaves were bursting green along the *Unter den Linden.* And everyone was laughing. And later we went boating on Lake Wannsee. You were so gallant, so handsome. You still are.

OTTO: Thank you, my love. You had such a pretty dress on. A sort of golden yellow. You were so beautiful. You still are. (*ANNE yawns.*)

EDITH: Go to bed!

ANNE: Yes, Mother. Soon. (*ANNE makes an entry into the diary. Bumps into a shirtless PETER who has been washing himself and hovering.*) Showing off again.

PETER: Showing off?

ANNE: If I had a body like that I wouldn't show it off.

PETER: You never talk to me properly. Why don't you like me?
(*Silence.*)
Can I see your diary?
(*Silence.*)
Am I in it?
(*Silence.*)
I'm intrigued.

ANNE: Look, Peter! Because we live in close proximity, we do not actually need to like each other. Or be involved in any way.

PETER: I agree. Goodnight.

ANNE: Goodnight.

MRS VAN DAAN: (*Seeing them.*) Peter! Bedtime!

PETER: Yes, Mother. Goodnight.

ANNE: You've said it already.

EDITH: I won't tell you again.

ANNE: Sorry, Mother. Just coming. Peter is not very good-looking. But he has such lovely eyes.

EDITH: Anne!

ANNE: Coming! (*But she does not go to bed.*) Funny thing, freedom. You take it for granted until you lose it.

OTTO: (*Mumbling from sleep.*) Anne! I order you to put away that diary. This instant!

ANNE: Yes, Father. Soon.

MARGOT: (*Calling across in a whisper.*) Anne! You awake?

ANNE: No!

MARGOT: Me also. I miss the snow. Being able to walk through snow.

ANNE: In my dreams I'm wandering through the softest, purest, finest snow you ever saw.
(*The visual effect is immediate.*)

MARGOT: Thank you. I can see it. Goodnight, Anne darling.

ANNE: Goodnight, Margot.
(*They settle down. But in the dark ANNE cries.*)

EDITH: (*Going to ANNE.*) There! There! My little darling! Everything will be alright! My lovely girl. I can still see you both when you were very small, and I can hear you, giggling in the golden sunlight, building castles upon the sandbanks of time. You both wore beautiful white dresses and gorgeous floppy hats. And we took you both to Berlin long before you know who came to power, we sat outside a café in the *Unter den Linden*, just watching the passers-by. Somehow or other it seems like another universe. *Unter den Linden.* Under the lime trees. Mad, audacious Berlin. Such a beautiful city. City of chestnut blossom. And not a slogan, not a murderous look in sight. (*Almost cries.*)

ANNE: (*Comforting her.*)Thank you, Mother, for being you.
(*EDITH kisses ANNE and goes back to bed.*)

EDITH: Goodnight.

ALL: (*Sing.*)

HELPING HAND,

PLEASE HELP ME.

KNOCK ON MY DOOR,

BRING ME GOOD NEWS.

HELPING HAND,
PLEASE HELP ME.
BRING ME SOME HOPE.
OPEN THE WAY.

UNLOCK THIS DARK,
THROW AWAY HATE.

HELPING HAND,
PLEASE HELP ME.
HOLD THE TORCH HIGH.
SAVE US IN TIME.

TOUCH PEOPLE'S HEARTS,
TURN ON THEIR LOVE

TAKE UP THE SWORD,
SLASH AWAY CLOUD.

ENTER OUR LIVES,
LIFT US IN TIME.

(*There is a sudden noise outside and a crash. They all freeze.*)

MARGOT: Are we betrayed?

OTTO: Leave this to me.

(*OTTO carefully creeps and slowly opens the door. At first there is silence. But then there is the sudden wild cry and screech of a cat. Everyone jumps. OTTO returns relieved.*)

A cat. Just a mangy, old Tom-cat, on the prowl, looking for his girlfriend.

(*Relief. Jollity. They all sing a last reprise of 'Helping Hand'.*)

ALL: (*Sing.*)

HELPING HAND,
PLEASE HELP US.
BRING THE WORLD PEACE.
BRING THE WORLD PEACE.
HELPING HAND
PLEASE HELP ME.

End of Act One.

ACT TWO

Departure

Scene 1

All enter and assemble as if asleep. Music starts and one by one they begin dancing.

OTTO enters with the diary and puts it down.

The music stops.

Scene 2

ANNE: (*Clutching her diary.*) August the fourth, 1944. The war is almost over and Germany is losing. The end cannot be that far away.

MARGOT: It wouldn't be a bad idea if you gave us a helping hand sometimes.

MRS VAN DAAN: Hear! Hear!

PETER: (*Exercising.*) Anne works harder than all of us. In her mind.

MR VAN DAAN: Yes. Leave her alone. She's only a child. What does she know of the world?

MR DUSSEL: I don't object to her diary, as long as it is rational, truthful and objective.

ANNE: Truth is never objective. We all have our own version. If you wore a hat I would say you are talking out of it.

MRS VAN DAAN: How could you allow her to speak like that to you?

ANNE: Thus another day passes. And another day. Days merge into days. A daze of days. No real signposts. Just days and days and days.

MR VAN DAAN: Would you like to hear a joke?

MR DUSSEL: No thank you.

MR VAN DAAN: It'll kill you. Hitler was on his horse, riding down the centre of Berlin, his legions behind him.

The horse slipped and Hitler fell off and would have
fallen on his head and probably died of a brain injury, if
a little man on the pavement hadn't rushed forward and
somehow, bravely managed to break Der Führer's fall.
'How can I thank you?' Hitler said. 'What is your name?'
The little man replied, 'Solomon Cohen.' Hitler was
surprised. 'But you're a Jew!' 'What else?' said the little
man. 'Never mind,' Hitler said, 'you acted with extreme
courage and I would like to grant you anything you
desire. Anything.' The man thought for a moment.
'Anything? Please! Not a word of this to anyone.'
(*Nobody laughs.*)
Isn't that fantastically funny?
(*Again he meets with a blank response.*)
I can sing too. I'm as good as Eddie Cantor or Al Jolson,
even if I do say so myself. Listen. (*Gets down on one knee.*)
'Climb upon my knee, Sonny Boy, though you're sixty-
three, Sonny Boy.'

MRS VAN DAAN: Eat your breakfast. It's getting cold.

PETER: (*Joins ANNE.*) You are the watcher. The witness.

ANNE: Writing helps me pass the time. It gives me
a purpose. It's everything.

PETER/ANNE: (*Sing.*)

WHEN THE WAR IS OVER
WE'LL FLY TO SAMARKAND
AND CROSS THE GOBI DESERT
FIND TREASURE IN THE SAND.

WHEN THE WAR IS OVER
I'LL RUSH OUT IN THE STREET
AND CHAT WITH EVERYBODY
AND LIFE WILL BE COMPLETE.

WHEN THE WAR IS OVER
WE'LL DRIVE TO KATMANDU
AND SWIM IN CORAL OCEANS,
CLIMB PYRAMIDS IN PERU.

WHEN THE WAR IS OVER
I'LL JUST WALK IN THE RAIN,

EAT A TOFFEE APPLE,
SEE MY HOUSE AGAIN.

WHEN THE WAR IS OVER
WE'LL CLIMB MOUNT EVEREST
AND THEN FLY OFF TO AFRICA
OUR LIVES AN ENDLESS QUEST.

WHEN THE WAR IS OVER
I'LL PADDLE IN THE SEA
LICKING CHOCOLATE ICE CREAM
AND HAVE MY FRIENDS TO TEA.

YES! WHEN THE WAR IS OVER
AND NICENESS IS THE RULE
WE'LL GET OUR BOOKS TOGETHER
AND THEN WE'LL GO TO SCHOOL.

WHEN THE WAR IS OVER –
WHEN THE WAR IS OVER –

PETER: You never stop. What is there to write about?

ANNE: The diary opens my mind. I can explore myself.
My hidden self. I remove myself from monotony. I can
dream. Let's go.

PETER: Where?

ANNE: Quickly! Hop aboard my dream.

PETER: I'm there already.

Scene 3

In the Black Forest.

ANNE: Why does everyone always pick on me? If I'm silent,
I'm sulking. If I'm writing, I'm being aloof, mysterious. If
I talk, I'm cheeky. They say I cause all the trouble. But
I'm never, never to blame.

PETER: Never! We're in a forest.

ANNE: In the forest of my brain. Who am I? Which way
did I go? I don't know who I am.

PETER: If I kiss you, you'll know who you are.

ANNE: Ssssh. This is the Black Forest where good German
folk live.

PETER: Are there any?

ANNE: Slowly. We mustn't kill crocuses. Stop a moment. Don't you love spring? Tiny flowers; peeping through the hard earth. Each one a miracle. Yellow, mauve crocus. Snowdrop. Primrose. Violet. And look! Trees are more beautiful than people. No! That's not true. People are the most beautiful things in the whole of creation. Why have you stopped walking?

PETER: What are we doing in the Black Forest?

ANNE: What are we doing in life? Creep!

PETER: I'm not a creep. I'm very nice. Taste me.

ANNE: We must be careful or the witch will get us.

PETER: Let me put my arm around you?

ANNE: I prefer the witch.

PETER: Do you like me?

ANNE: Not much.

PETER: That makes two of us. Goodbye. (*He goes.*)

ANNE: I was only joking. Come back. Please! I wish he'd come back. He's got such a nice smile. Why are boys so stupid? I don't like being alone.

MRS VAN DAAN: (*As witch. Wearing a potty on her head.*) You're not alone. Welcome to my gingerbread house. (*A gingerbread house arrives.*)

ANNE: How beautiful. It smells so fresh. It's still warm. May I go inside?

MRS VAN DAAN: (*As witch.*) It's all yours. (*ANNE enters the house.*)

ANNE: It's very hot in here. Are you coming in?

MRS VAN DAAN: (*As witch.*) Presently.

ANNE: May I come out now?

MRS VAN DAAN: (*As witch.*) No. Stay. You are the chosen. You'll get used to it.

ANNE: I'm afraid. And hungry.

MRS VAN DAAN: (*As witch.*) Then eat the house.

ANNE: Thank you. Can I eat the doorknob?

MRS VAN DAAN: (*As witch.*) Be my guest. Lick the mirror. It's honey toffee. (*ANNE starts to eat.*) There's the oven over there. Where it all happens.

ANNE: Yum. Yum.

MRS VAN DAAN: (*As witch.*) What are you writing, Anne, all the time?

ANNE: Words. Just words.

MRS VAN DAAN: (*As witch.*) A great epic, I'm sure. You might become famous. The world at your feet.

ANNE: Poor world. I wouldn't like to be at my feet.

MRS VAN DAAN: (*As witch.*) But none of us will know of course.

ANNE: I know. How sad.

MRS VAN DAAN: (*As witch.*) How old are you?

ANNE: Funny, you're a witch, but I'm not afraid of you. I'm fourteen.

MRS VAN DAAN: (*As witch.*) What would you like more than anything else in the world?

ANNE: To be fifteen. To be ordinary. To live a quiet life. To be famous. To go everywhere. I'm confused. Strange things are happening inside me. You see, I want to grow up.

MRS VAN DAAN: (*As witch.*) Well, eat then. You couldn't have come to a better place. Nothing like a gingerbread house to clear up confusion. This oven solves everything. The best German firms tendered for it and it's very efficient. Eat! Eat! There's a lot of Jews waiting to be admitted. Gingerbread and hard work makes free. Look! Maybe they can help you.

(*All people from the attic appear.*)

ANNE: Mother! Margot! (*Cuddles them.*)

MARGOT: What are you doing?

ANNE: Eating this gingerbread house, of course.

MR DUSSEL: May we join you?

ANNE: Be my guest.

EDITH: Dig in, everyone. It's not rationed. Enjoy.

MR VAN DAAN: I'm famished.

OTTO: Sweet for the sweet.

(*They all get on all fours and ravenously start to eat the house.*)

EDITH: Where are we?

ANNE: The enchanted forest. Where you meet yourself and come face to face with your future. Where's Peter!

PETER: I love you. I am death. And you are mine. Forever. Come.

ANNE: Help me! Help me!

ALL: (*Sing.*) 'Who's afraid of the big bad wolf? The big bad wolf. The big bad wolf. Who's afraid of the big bad wolf? Tra la la la la – '

Scene 4

MARGOT: Thank you. Thank you. And now we bring you the Andrew's Sisters!

(*MARGOT, EDITH and MRS VAN DAAN sing 'Yes, My Darling Daughter'. ANNE screams.*)

ANNE: HELP ME! HELP ME! MOTHER! HELP ME!

EDITH: (*Rushing to her.*) Anne! Darling!

ANNE: Where am I?

EDITH: Having a nasty nightmare. You're alright.

ANNE: Please go back to the others. Peter, I ran away from you. But when you weren't there I looked for you.

PETER: The things you run away from you run right into.

(*Anti-aircraft shells and bomb sounds reverberate.*)

ANNE: The war outside is going well.

PETER: Yes. It will all be over soon.

ANNE: (*Shivers.*) I'm scared.

PETER: We're all scared. We have a right to be. I like you a lot.

ANNE: I know.

PETER: I like you very much. Anne! Say something.

ANNE: The war will be over soon.

PETER: I don't ever want another girlfriend.

ANNE: Oh?

PETER: You've got plenty of words for your diary, but so few for me.

ANNE: Jealous?

PETER: Yes.

ANNE: You've got very nice eyes.

PETER: You think so? I think I – I lo – like you.

ANNE: Good.

PETER: Did you say 'Good'? (*Turns cartwheels.*)

ANNE: Quiet! Keep it secret.

(*PETER is about to kiss ANNE, but at the last moment lacks the courage.*)

MRS VAN DAAN: (*Calling.*) Peter!

PETER: If only we could escape. For always.

(*ANNE searches for a doll. Finds it.*)

ANNE: Marguerite! There you are! Where have you been, you naughty girl? (*Holds the doll very tight.*) Sad really. Suddenly I'm too old for you. And I'm too young for babies.

OTTO: (*Comes and touches her gently.*) You alright?

ANNE: I'm fine.

OTTO: Don't worry, my darling. Everything's alright. You were just having a bad dream.

ANNE: I know. I was so afraid in that dream. I was looking everywhere for my lost childhood. I hate being shut up here. But I must write. And I must dream.

OTTO: Is this all a dream?

ANNE: Yes.

OTTO: Then dream this. Your mother and I care for you so much, now and forever, even in the darkest corners of your dream.

ANNE: Thank you.

OTTO: Tell you what isn't a dream. The fact that you are special. And something wonderful will happen to you.

ANNE: What do you mean?

OTTO: I'm not sure. There's no logic in faith. But we're all going to be so proud of you.

ANNE: What will we do after the war?

OTTO: First we'll go on holiday. To the coast. To Blankenberg. Or maybe to Paris or London and see all the sights. Big Ben. Buckingham Palace, the Eiffel Tower! The Arc de Triomphe. But for now, all we have is an attic above Amsterdam, so I must go back to the others. Be good and you'll be happy tomorrow.

ANNE: I'm happy tonight. Very happy. I might be in love.

OTTO: I know. We're not blind. But boys can spell trouble.

ANNE: Peter's different.

OTTO: Anne! Please stop dreaming.

ANNE: I'll try. Daddy! What will become of us?

(*OTTO smiles and floats away.*)

Scene 5

The other people fade. ANNE gets an idea. Jazz music plays.

ANNE: Come on, Peter. Are you coming or not?

PETER: Aye, aye, captain.

ANNE: We've raised anchor. Jump aboard.

PETER: Where we sailing?

ANNE: To the future.

PETER: In that case don't go without me.

ANNE: All aboard the *Rotterdam*. The huge ocean liner. We are all at sea.

PETER: And the moon on the water and you in my arms. Shall we canoodle?

ANNE: Land ahoy! We're there!

PETER: Where?

ANNE: Hollywood, of course.

(*All become smiling dwarfs except for MRS VAN DAAN who is the wicked queen.*)

ALL: 'HIGH-HO! HIGH-HO! TO HOLLYWOOD WE GO.' (*They continue the song by whistling together.*)

ANNE: Snow White was the most beautiful princess, but somehow she wasn't real, not flesh and blood.

MRS VAN DAAN: (*As queen.*) Mirror, mirror on the wall, who is the prettiest, nastiest of them all? You are! Come over here!

ANNE: Careful! The wicked queen!

(*PETER automatically goes towards his mother.*)

Where you going?

PETER: Don't worry. I'll settle her.

ANNE: Goodbye, Peter.

PETER: Mother! I must tell you something.

MRS VAN DAAN: (*As queen.*) Sit down.

(*PETER obeys and MRS VAN DAAN sits on him.*)

PETER: Mother! I'm in love...

(*ANNE and MARGOT sing 'I'm Wishing' from 'Snow-White'.*)

PETER: I'm in love with Anne.

MARGOT: I can see that Peter is just perfect for you, Anne. You have my blessing.

ANNE: Thank you. This is a dream and a half.

OTTO: Right! Let's wrap this up.

EDITH: All we want is a happy ending.

ANNE: Ladies and gentlemen. I have an important announcement to make. Peter and I are getting married.

(*ANNE and MARGOT embrace.*)

PETER: Are we?

ANNE: Yes.

PETER: When?

ANNE: Now. Right now.

PETER: Are we?

ANNE: I love you.

MARGOT: He'll make a beautiful brother-in-law.

ANNE: (*To MARGOT.*) I'm so happy.

(*The sisters embrace and the scene darkens as the people make improvised musical wedding sounds. ANNE takes a sheet from her bed and wraps it around her, improvising a wedding gown. The women get another sheet and the four parents raise it above their heads, each holding a corner. This becomes a wedding canopy. ANNE conducts up the air and brings about Mendelssohn's Wedding March.*)

Stars! Trees! The full moon, my crown. Look!

(*The dark becomes a mass of stars. The bells sound happily.*)

The whole universe witness to our wedding. And even God is somewhere quite close. Can't you smell him?

(*They all sniff.*)

EDITH: Just smoke. I can just smell smoke.

(*PETER and ANNE stand together under the canopy. MR DUSSEL becomes a cantor, sings a wedding prayer, holds up a wine glass, places it under PETER's foot.*)

MR DUSSEL: To remind us of the destruction of the temple.

ANNE: We've got long memories. Smash it, Peter.

(*He does.*)

ALL: MAZELTOV. GOOD LUCK.

(*OTTO and MR VAN DAAN embrace and start a slow eastern European dance.*)

MEN: 'CHOSAN CHOLA MAZELTOV – DADA – DEEDEE – DADADA – '

(*The others join in but ANNE commands them to freeze as she and PETER dance slowly together.*)

ANNE: What about the wedding feast?

PETER: You are the wedding feast.

(*Everyone else is seated for a meal. But the wedding is over. We are back to our reality of the attic.*)

EDITH: Come and get it! Tulip bulb and potato soup!

PETER: Dreams are over. Back to who we are. Back to where we are.

Scene 6

ANNE: Amsterdam. August the fourth, 1944.

(*Air-raid outside.*)

EDITH: The war is nearly over and we shall be free.

ANNE: Free?

EDITH: What?

ANNE: Nothing. (*Smiles, trying to hide her foreboding.*)

EDITH: Tell me the truth. What do you see?

ANNE: I see peace. Perfect and beautiful peace. And I love you both, forever. (*Hugs OTTO and EDITH.*)

EDITH: Soup! Soup! Who wants soup?

MRS VAN DAAN: Lunchtime. Come and get it.

(*The others eat.*)

Join in, Anne! That's your trouble. You never join in.

PETER: This soup is wonderful. Ugh!

EDITH: Lunch will do for supper tomorrow, so let's all have breakfast tonight.

MARGOT: After this war and the end of this nightmare, I want to go out into the streets of Amsterdam and kiss the very first handsome young man I meet and fall in love and get married and have five children.

MRS VAN DAAN: You'll be lucky.

MARGOT: I've not given up hope. Where there's life there's hope. And I know that all this will soon be a thing of the past and we'll get on and live our lives to the full.

PETER: Eat! That's my philosophy. Eat while you can. Live for the moment.

ANNE: Boys! All they think about. Their stomachs.

(PETER is lost in eating. ANNE goes to leave.)

EDITH: Where you going, darling?

ANNE: I need fresh air. I need to escape. I need to see my beautiful city. Just once more. I need to stretch and breathe the sky.

EDITH: *(Humouring her.)* Yes, darling. Don't we all.

(ANNE tries the trap door.)

Darling. What are you doing?

(ANNE sings 'Dancing in the Dark' and floats into an empty square. Night. Amsterdam. There are searchlights and the crump of bombs.)

Come, bombs! Come, fire! Devour the Nazi monster. Even destroy my beloved Amsterdam if you have to.

(She sings 'Outside Inside'.)

OUTSIDE INSIDE

TWO WORLDS APART

INSIDE WE ARGUE

OUTSIDE WE PART

INSIDE WE'RE SAFE

BUT WE FIGHT FOR A CHAIR

OUTSIDE WE'RE TAKEN

TO GOD KNOWS WHERE

OUTSIDE INSIDE

TWO WORLDS APART

INSIDE WE ARGUE

OUTSIDE THE BROKEN HEART

AND SKY AND TRAVEL AND DEATH.

(Outside the Royal Palace. A man, played by MR DUSSEL, stalks her.)

MR DUSSEL: *(As man.)* What are you doing in the streets, child? In the middle of the night?

ANNE: Looking for my childhood.

MR DUSSEL: (*As man.*) But surely you want to grow up.

ANNE: Yes. But I'm afraid. I want life to go backward.

MR DUSSEL: (*As man.*) Ah yes, I thought you were in pain. Can I tell you about my hobby? I am totally obsessed with military bands. I would follow any band, good or bad, to the ends of the earth and often do in my imagination. As soon as I get home I immediately start the military music on my radiogram. I know every march ever written, almost every band that ever played, their particular style. There in my living room I march, back and forth, back and forth, every lunchtime, every night. It is wonderful exercise and I can assure you it is a morally uplifting and spiritual experience. The Germans are a humane race, compassionate. I know you are afraid because of the things you have heard they have done or are about to do. A lot of this you can disregard. It is propaganda. I maintain that soon you will notice a big change. An occupying power is bound to take actions that seem draconian and excessively harsh early on. The Jews were merely an expediency, a scapegoat for our ambitions. It is almost understandable, even if a little painful. Open up. (*MR DUSSEL has become Hitler and wants to probe into ANNE's mouth.*) Where's my scalpel?

ANNE: Here! (*She takes the knife from his white coat pocket, thrusts it into his stomach.*)

MR DUSSEL: Help me. Help me. Hel – (*He raises his arm calling to her, but his cry becomes Hitler's fanatical call to his followers.*) HEIL! HEIL!
(*Mass crowds shout 'Heil' in reply.*)

ANNE: Hitler's dead.
(*ANNE is by the radio and EDITH comes.*)

EDITH: What are you doing up, this time of night?

ANNE: Mother! (*She whispers in EDITH's ear.*)

EDITH: What?

ANNE: It's true! It's true!

EDITH: What are you saying?
(*ANNE again whispers into her ear.*)
How do you know?

ANNE: It must be true. It must be so. They announced it on the radio.

EDITH: IT'S WONDERFUL! WAKE UP, EVERYONE! IT'S WONDERFUL!

(*MRS VAN DAAN emerges from sleep.*)

MRS VAN DAAN: What's happening?

EDITH: It's true. (*She whispers into MRS VAN DAAN's ear.*)

MRS VAN DAAN: WHAT? Are you sure?

EDITH: It's true!

MRS VAN DAAN: How do you know?

EDITH: Anne heard it on the radio. It's official!

(*MRS VAN DAAN kisses EDITH and dances with her.*)

MRS VAN DAAN: WAKE UP, EVERYONE! WAKE UP. IT'S TRUE. IT'S OFFICIAL.

(*One by one the rest emerge from sleep, yawning and still barely comprehending.*)

ALL: What is it? Is it the end of the world?

MRS VAN DAAN: It's wonderful. It's unbelievable. It's official.

MR DUSSEL: Wait! How do we know it's true?

ALL: Yes! How do we know? How do we know?

EDITH: It must be true. It must be so. She heard it on the radio.

ANNE: It must be true. It must be so. I heard it on the radio.

(*ALL now move ritualistically, building up to a climax, the song spurring them on.*)

ALL: (*Sing.*)

HITLER IS DEAD!

HITLER IS DEAD!

SHOT IN THE HEAD.

BUTCHERED IN BED.

MAGGOTS ARE CRAWLING

INSIDE HIS HEAD.

HIS EYEBALLS ARE JELLY,

HE'S SKEWERED THROUGH THE BELLY.

HE'S MANGLED AND MINCED

AND WE ARE CONVINCED

THAT HITLER IS DEAD.

HITLER IS DEAD. HITLER IS DEAD.

STRANGLED IN BED.

STRANGLED IN BED.

THEY'VE SAWN OFF HIS THIGHS,

SUCKED OUT HIS EYES.

SLUGS IN HIS SOCKETS,

RATS IN HIS POCKETS.

BATTERED AND SHATTERED,

SHATTERED AND BATTERED.

THEY'VE SCATTERED HIS HEAD,

HIS FINGERS, HIS TOES.

HIS HEART, HIS NOSE.

HIS FINGERS, HIS TOES,

HIS HEART, HIS NOSE.

HITLER IS DEAD! DEAD!

DEAD! DEAD!

DEAD DEAD DEAD. DEAD!

(*When the song ends they are drained, shattered.*)

Scene 7

MR VAN DAAN: Let's celebrate! I've been saving something special.

(*They laugh as MR VAN DAAN brings out a bottle of wine from his secret hiding place.*)

Are we sure? Who heard this news?

ANNE: I did. On the radio.

MR VAN DAAN: (*Looking down through the trap door.*) Nothing's different in the street.

MR DUSSEL: (*Twiddling radio.*) Everything's the same. Nothing's new. It's not true.

EDITH: Anne, is it true?

OTTO: Is it true? Is it true?

ANNE: It must be true. He must be dead. I want him to be dead. Dad! Mummy! Please let him be dead.

(*EDITH whispers to OTTO.*)

MRS VAN DAAN: Liar! Liar! How could you do this to us? (*Suddenly she attacks ANNE, pulling her hair.*)

MR VAN DAAN: (*Trying to restrain his wife.*) Angel face! Please!

EDITH: She's only a child. She's only a child! It was a joke. You understand jokes.

MR VAN DAAN: It was a bad joke, Anne. The time for jokes is over.

EDITH: (*Strokes her crying daughter's hair.*) Take no notice, darling. She means well but she's stupid.

MRS VAN DAAN: Me? Stupid? Did you call me stupid?

OTTO: Silence! Or we'll be discovered.

(*They all start whispering.*)

MRS VAN DAAN: This is the worst thing that ever happened to me. This dreaming, thinking and writing. It leads to trouble. It should be stopped. That girl should face reality.

OTTO: Anne, she's right. You must stop dreaming.

ANNE: Without dreams what are we?

EDITH: Anne! I understand. But we all have to grow up.

ANNE: Look what the grown-ups have done to this world. Hitler must be dead. He must be dead.

MRS VAN DAAN: (*Angrily.*) Peter! Stay away from her.

PETER: Yes, Mother.

OTTO: Stay away from him.

ANNE: Yes, Father

MR VAN DAAN: We mean it, young man! And go to bed.

PETER: Yes, Father. I love you, Anne. Forever.

ANNE: I love you until the end of the world.

PETER: And this is true and not a dream.

ANNE: But dreams are also true. The truth of your deep inner self.

PETER: You're writing all this down, aren't you?

ANNE: Yes.

PETER: Read your diary to me. Please. All of it. Now.

ANNE: No one else must ever read my diary. My secrets. My truth.

PETER: Am I in your diary?

ANNE: What do you think?

PETER: Please show me your diary.

ANNE: Now?

PETER: Now. Please

ANNE: I must tell you this. I love you with this kiss. (*They kiss.*) At least we have this.

PETER: At least we have this. I love you with this kiss. (*They kiss again.*)

ANNE: I would have loved a lifetime of this.

(*ANNE opens her diary. A terrible wind blows. All the doors fly open. The diary flies out of her hand.*)

ANNE: No. Not yet! I haven't finished yet. (*She sings.*)

HELPING HAND!

PLEASE HELP ME.

TURN BACK THE CLOCK.

SAVE US IN TIME.

PETER: What's happening?

ANNE: We are betrayed.

PETER: How? Who?

(*The door comes off its hinges. Smoke pours in. German voices.*)

ANNE: Does it matter now? We're going on a journey.

(*Suddenly we hear people rushing upstairs. Shouting, spiralling, echoing voices.*)

VOICES: *RAUS! RAUS! JUDEN RAUS! SCHNELL! SCHNELL!*

(*Menacing sounds drown everything. Then silence and blinding light.*)

PETER: I love you, Anne. To the end of the world.

ANNE: I love you forever, Peter. 'Til the beginning of time. Funny. Just as my world opens, it closes. Just as I stop being a child I stop being. In my beginning is my end. Hold me. Hold me! Hold me! Trains. I hear trains. (*Train sounds.*)

Night and fog. Night and fog.

(*Fog envelops them and in the darkness a thin light shines on everyone. They have become a mass, a sort of boxcar. We concentrate on each face in turn.*)

MRS VAN DAAN: Why?

MR VAN DAAN: Why?

MARGOT: Why?

EDITH: Why?

OTTO: Why?

PETER: Why?
MR DUSSEL: Why?

Scene 8

The earlier knocking on the door has now become the sound of trains wailing, chugging. They all wear yellow stars and now they become a mass, as if wedged together, not only in a boxcar but actually becoming a moving boxcar.

ANNE: Dreams are over. The nightmare starts. Night and fog. Night and fog. Night and fog.
(Throughout this train scene ANNE continues to repeat this litany.)
MR DUSSEL: Why are humans doing this to humans? Why?
MRS VAN DAAN: Goodbye! Goodbye. Goodbye, Amsterdam.
MR VAN DAAN: Goodbye, world. Family. Friends.
MARGOT: We didn't ask much from life. We just wanted to live it.
EDITH: Remember us. Bear witness.
OTTO: This is the end of the end of the end.
MARGOT: Who will remember us? Who will know we were here?
(They undress to reveal identical prison camp clothing, then they join tight together and sway and chant a prayer, as if they have only one identity.)
ALL: 'A-NI MA-MIN. A-NI MA-MIN. AN-I MA-MIN. Be-e-mu-no shiel mo be-vi-as, Ha-mo-shi-ach-be-vi-as ha-mo-shi-ach a-ni ma min-ve af al pi she yis ma-me-ach im kol zeh a-ni ma-min'.
(They exit through the back door. ANNE alone remains.)
ANNE: *(Chanting, translating the gist of their final prayer.)*
'I believe that the Messiah will come. And even though he is a little late I will still believe.' People of the world. Save us. Before it's too late. I'm trying to hear your voice, your protest. Children of the world, remember

me. I was born. I lived for a while. I fell in love and then I went back again into the dark. (*She dances.*) Life is the beautiful light in the entire darkness of time. I dance. Dance because I believe that I exist and I love and I will exist and love forever. Against all the odds. We are beautiful, and yes, we are loving. And we will love one another. One day. All of us. Everywhere. You'll see. Before I go down into the dark, into the night and fog, please remember me. And peace will come. And a thousand centuries of leaves and wind and rain and snow will cover the snow, again and again. And people will come and go. And fall in love. And peace will come. And peace will come. Goodbye, Diary.

DIARY: Goodbye, Anne! I have all your words inside me. And I will sing of you. And you will never die.

(*ANNE kisses her diary and reluctantly discards it, putting it down upon the pile of clothes heaped on the stage, and she exits through the back door, following the others. Her diary seems to light up the darkness that now envelops everything.*)

Scene 9

OTTO enters.

OTTO: We were in that attic for two years. Until we were betrayed. And then we were taken on that terrible journey, to Auschwitz, where millions of us died, by gas. The war was almost over. Margot and Anne were moved to Germany. It was March, 1945. Anne was fifteen. There, in Bergen-Belsen, Margot and Anne died from typhus. Desolate. Alone. Their spirit gone. A few weeks later the German army surrendered. It was that close. Irony. Anyway, it was all over. All our children went up together, into that exodus, into the clouds, leaving us behind, with dreams, memories, fragments of time. But sometimes I can hear their laughter upon the wind. Her book is special, yet what can replace the laughter of a living child? Anne's book is a marvel, because it contains and captures the hopes and the dreams and the fears of a girl who bore witness to the fact that we were here. That we were cut off and denied our lives, so cruelly. But words are inadequate. This book is precious, yet it is only a book and life is the most precious thing of all. All the books ever written cannot be weighed against the value of one child's life. I would gladly swap it, throw it away, or have it unwritten if I could only have Anne again, living.

(*He closes the diary. The stage goes dark.*)

The End.

ON MARGATE SANDS

Characters

BRIAN

LARRY

DOLORES

MICHELLE

BUZZ

PRIEST

JOAN KILLICK

JOHN KILLICK

On Margate Sands was first performed by CV1 at the Arts Centre, Nottingham in October 1980 with the following cast:

BRIAN, Bill Stewart

LARRY, Alan Collins

DOLORES, Cotchie D'Arcy

MICHELLE, Tamara Steele

BUZZ, Tony Portacio

PRIEST, Simon Shaw

JOAN KILLICK, Caroline Hunt

JOHN KILLICK, Rod Lewis

Director, Ron Pember

Setting: the esplanade and beach. Margate. Winter.

ACT ONE

The beach. A dark, bitter cold day. The sea is rough. Several people are hanging about the beach. We notice two in particular: one is very young and the other is quite old. This is LARRY, the young one is BUZZ. BUZZ starts searching around, beach-combing in a small area, picking up various objects, biting on them, and chucking them away again. Then he finds an armless and legless, cheap, smiling doll. He throws this up into the air several times and catches it. Then he holds the face to LARRY's chest as if trying to make it suckle from the older man's nipple. LARRY gives BUZZ a clip and the boy tucks the doll into his inside pocket.

Wandering about the beach is BRIAN, carrying a cassette and old suitcase. He smiles at everybody, occasionally saying 'good morning.' There is no response. He sees a telephone and lifts the receiver.

BRIAN: Hello? Hello? Anyone there? (*Then he sees the printed instructions on the notice before him. He repeats the instructions.*) For… operator… lift receiver… and dial… one hundred… one... zero... zero… Oh hello, miss… I want to trace my sister… she lives in Southampton. Yes. Yes. Wait… one… nine… two. Directory Enquiries? Thank… thank you. One… nine… two. One… nine… two. One… nine… two. (*Now he dials the number.*) Yes, please. My name is Brian Singleton. I want to contact my sister. She lives in Southampton. In Hampshire. Sorry… if I knew her address, I wouldn't need to ask you. You're Enquiries, not me. (*The line goes dead but he still talks to the receiver.*) I just wanted to tell her that I'm out and arrived safely in Margate. (*Sings 'Chattanooga Choochoo' quietly.*)
(*LARRY strikes a match and starts a fire. BUZZ blows and blows upon the flames and holds his hands to the fire contentedly. They settle. BUZZ takes out a monster comic and starts to read. LARRY breaks up several dog-ends, rolls two cigarettes and lights them, one for himself and one for BUZZ. BUZZ takes the cigarette, takes one puff and eats the rest of the cigarette. Then he lights a piece of paper and runs the flame lovingly along his hand.*)

DOLORES: (*Off.*) Yoohoo! Yoohoo!

LARRY: Oh, Gawd!

DOLORES: (*Off.*) We can see you!

(*Someone is waving frantically from the esplanade. This is DOLORES, over made-up, overdressed, overweight. She is accompanied by a quiet, anorexic-looking young girl. This is MICHELLE, who hardly ever speaks, but sometimes repeats the words from other people's sentences. DOLORES, followed by MICHELLE approaches.*)

DOLORES: Hello, darling. Hello, love!

(*She is ignored.*)

Thought you'd come straight here. Mind if I join you? Lovely fire. Can I help myself?

LARRY: Flames is free.

DOLORES: Guess what I fancy? Guess what I feel like? Oooooh. (*Squeezes her legs together.*) Guess what I suddenly fancy? (*Lies back and opens her legs.*) Ooh yes, I need it. More than medicine. It's my antidote to old age.

(*LARRY sniggers.*)

I could do with it five times a day after meals if there was a man around to give it to me. Why not? Passes the time. Passes the time.

(*BUZZ gives MICHELLE the doll. She kisses it and throws it away.*)

What time is it anyway? (*She takes an alarm clock out of her bag.*) Shite! Two hours till dinner. Two whole hours out in this hole. This arsehole, this pisshouse of a town. If only she'd let us in for once. (*She shouts towards town.*) Mrs Killick, you cow! Cow! I'll pull your intestines out. I'll slit you from your bung hole to your tongue hole. You'll get yours, Mrs Killick! You cow.

MICHELLE: Cow. Cow.

DOLORES: Wonder what's for supper tonight. Shall we go home? Shall we chance it? You're right. Useless. Got to be the end of the world before she'd let us in. Mind you… (*Takes out a newspaper and shoves it under LARRY's nose.*) According to this we ain't got that much longer to wait. (*Shivers.*) Ooh, cuts right through yer. Fancy

a cuddle? Care for a cuddle? (*No takers.*) Give us
a cuddle, Michelle.
(*MICHELLE smiles.*)
MICHELLE: Cuddle Michelle.
(*She goes over to DOLORES. They hug and cuddle. It is
an act of friendship, of human warmth. LARRY has been
dozing off. BUZZ lights a match and slowly approaches
LARRY with the flame. He holds the flame to LARRY's
foot, trying to set the shoe alight. LARRY leaps up and
hops around. Everyone else laughs. LARRY grabs BUZZ
by the throat, then he slaps the boy around the face, first
one side and then the other. BUZZ continues smiling as if
nothing is happening.*)
LARRY: What are you doing, you stupid sod! Don't ever do
that again, mate! Understand? Be last thing you ever did.
Understand?
(*BUZZ nods, smiling. DOLORES rushes over and LARRY
cringes away.*)
DOLORES: Leave him alone, you lousy bully. Leave my
lovely boy alone. (*Rubs BUZZ's hair.*) A rub for luck.
I have a rub every day, don't I, Buzz?
BUZZ: (*Quietly.*) I'll kill the bastard. One day I'll kill
the bastard.
LARRY: Alright. Alright. Sorry, Buzz. Didn't mean nothing.
(*The wind howls and BUZZ howls and they shiver and
huddle together.*)
LARRY: (*More to himself.*) That's it you see, bloody wind, it
sweeps down from Archangel, across the land mass of
Scandinavia, it cuts through the Skaggerrak, skims over
the North Sea and hits Margate smack on.
(*MICHELLE starts to whimper.*)
DOLORES: Did you take your pill?
(*MICHELLE nods.*)
Did you take your happy tab this morning?
(*MICHELLE nods.*)
Sure? Didn't hide it under your tongue and throw
it away?
(*MICHELLE shakes her head.*)
Good girl. Why you crying then?

(*DOLORES wipes MICHELLE's nose. A quiet descends.
They crouch round the fire. Out of the silence they notice
BRIAN. He rises and walks over to them.*)

BRIAN: Good morning. Good afternoon. Quite nice for
the time of year. Bit fresh, though. My sister's name is
Jeanette Singleton, though she might be calling herself
Jeanette Smithson by now. She's quite a famous actress,
I believe. Mind if I warm my hands?

DOLORES: Depends where you wanna warm them, darling.

LARRY: He's a nutter.

BRIAN: A traveller through life, you could say.

LARRY: He's aftercare.

BRIAN: I tried to contact my sister, tell her I am in
Margate. I just got off the coach I got on at Victoria
Coach Station.

LARRY: (*Muttering to the others.*) Another poor bugger
dumped here.

BRIAN: Dumped?

LARRY: In which looney bin have you bin?

BRIAN: Beg pardon?

LARRY: Alright. Which psychiatric hospital you bin
released from?

BRIAN: Nice to meet you.

(*MICHELLE smiles sweetly.*)

Good afternoon, miss... madam... How do you do?
My name is Brian Singleton.

(*He formally and stiffly shakes hands with MICHELLE
and DOLORES. The ladies enjoy the formality.*)

DOLORES: I'm Dolores.

BRIAN: That's a very nice name. It's exotic.

DOLORES: Yeah, 'spose so... I chose it myself when I took
on my new identity.

LARRY: Yeah, it's all titty with her!

(*LARRY and BUZZ laugh.*)

DOLORES: Filthy bastard. That's all you think about...
That's Larry, and he's Buzz. He loves fires.

BUZZ: I lit a really big fire in Basingstoke once.

BRIAN: (*Shaking hands again.*) How do you do?

BUZZ: Not sure.

LARRY: So where you from, mate?

BRIAN: It's wonderful here. (*Breathes deeply.*) The air's so fresh. I like Margate.

BUZZ: Mad-gate.

DOLORES: It's bloody cold. It's bloody freezing.

BRIAN: But it's a clean, healthy sort of cold.

LARRY: It's the arsehole of the year, mate. The dog-end. You are aftercare, ain't you?

DOLORES: Leave him alone.

LARRY: Don't worry, mate. We're all in the same boat or we were, but the boat's gone down. You can always tell people who's just come out. Always tell aftercare.

DOLORES: No after, no care. Just here and now. Who cares? What's this? (*Picks up a cassette player and turns it on.*) Rock 'n' Roll. (*Grabs MICHELLE, shows her the dance.*)

LARRY: How long were you in the loony bin?

BRIAN: Sorry! Do you happen to know this address, Collonade Hotel?

BARRY: (*Nudging BUZZ.*) What? No. Do we, Buzz? (*BUZZ shakes his head.*)

BRIAN: A Mrs Killick is the owner.

DOLORES: What? (*She takes the paper.*) What? Oh my Gawd, poor bugger…

BRIAN: Do you know her? I must go now… they're expecting me. Thank you very much for letting me share your fire.

LARRY: Hold on… did you say Collonade Hotel? Hang on, it's coming back… You cross over by the Parade. Take the first on the left by the traffic lights. Then the second on the right, Hazelhurst Road, first on the left, Hazelhurst Avenue and halfway along Collonade, can't miss it.

BRIAN: Thank you very much. I'm very obliged.

LARRY: You can trust us. Honest. Look at it this way. If you've been released, you've been declared sane.

BRIAN: I'm… I'm only concentrating on the future. It's wonderful to be here. The world's a wonderful place and

life's like a pilgrimage. It's like being born again.
Goodbye. (*He starts to walk away.*) Hope to see you again.

DOLORES: Bye, Brian. Best of luck.

MICHELLE: Best of luck.

BRIAN: Thank you. I'll need it. Toodle-oo. Cheerio.
Toodle-oo.

(*They all mimic him as he goes. They all laugh.*)

LARRY: How do you do?

DOLORES: Howdoyoudoyoudo...? Poor bugger. I really
feel sorry for him. You are a bastard, Larry, giving him
wrong directions. He'll get lost.

LARRY: He can't be more lost than he is.

DOLORES: Anyway, he's got lots of time, ain't he? It's the
one thing we've all got. (*Grabs MICHELLE again.*) Come
on, Rock 'n' Roll. Keep warm!

(*They dance. LARRY and BUZZ crouch around the fire. The
scene goes into dark.*)

BRIAN: (*Looking at the slip of paper, trying to memorise the
address.*) Collonade Hotel... Collon... Collon... ado...
Hotel... Mrs Killick, Proprietor. (*Then he sees the hotel
entrance and perks up.*) Collonade Hotel!

(*BRIAN rings the bell. The door is opened by a PRIEST who
is just leaving. The PRIEST has a quiet, pleasant voice. He
is always cheerful and friendly.*)

PRIEST: Hello! I was just on my way out. And you, it
appears, are just on your way in. You're a new guest
obviously.

BRIAN: Yes... my name is Brian Singleton... and I've just...
I just got off the coach...

PRIEST: I'm also quite new here in Margate, so we can
both settle in together.

BRIAN: Can I speak to the proprietor, please?

PRIEST: Certainly, ring the bell again. Unfortunately, I must
dash. Sorry, but we'll have a really nice heart to heart
later. Incidentally, I'm Reverend Robinson, but please call
me Mike. Think of me as a friend. I'm here to help you.
(*He leaves.*)

BRIAN: Thank you, sir.

(*He rings the bell again and LARRY opens the door wide. BUZZ is also there, laughing behind him.*)

LARRY: Can I help you?

BRIAN: You… But… ? (*He is surprised and confused.*) Can I see Mrs Killick, the proprietor, please?

LARRY: Ain't you surprised to see us?

BUZZ: Did you get lost?

BRIAN: Is Mrs Killick in please?

LARRY: Don't take umbrage, me old son, it was only a lark, wasn't it, Buzz?

BUZZ: Yeah, it was a lark.

LARRY: You worry too much, me old son. I can see that already.

BRIAN: I am not worried. I wish to see the proprietor.

LARRY: Come on. Come on in. Almost dinnertime.

BUZZ: Dinner! Dinner!

LARRY: Almost! Smells like rabbit, must be cat.

BUZZ: Cat giblets and rhubarb.

(*BRIAN goes inside. There appears to be lots of activity. He stands there with his cases, isolated and hunched into himself. Surrounded by the noise of many people, it is as if he is being jostled by a crowd of residents who are making their way from all directions to the dining room. BRIAN stands huddled against the wall.*

LARRY signals to BUZZ, and places BRIAN's suitcase just behind BRIAN's feet. BRIAN steps back and falls over. They laugh. Everyone around laughs.

JOAN KILLICK enters. She is a homely lady who smiles a lot. JOAN wears an over abundance of chunky jewellery and make-up. Her hair style is immaculate, tinted, slightly ridiculous and incongruous.)

JOAN: What's all this… ? You! What are you doing hanging about? How many times must I tell you? Idiot! Don't hang about the place. Understood?

(*LARRY cringes away from her anger but she then sees BRIAN and there is a dramatic change in her attitude.*)

Hello? Who are you then? You're Mr Singleton, aren't you? (*As if talking to a baby.*) You're Brian. You're late. We've been expecting you. Never mind, you're here now.

That's all that matters. Take off your wet things, love…
(*Helps BRIAN with his coat. He responds to her kindness.*)
Oh dear, oh dear, you're wet through. This is Brian,
everyone, our new guest. And just in time for dinner,
isn't that nice? Come on, don't dawdle. Stuffed dummies!
Christ, they'd try the patience of a bloody saint. Stinking
filthy creatures… (*Shudders.*) That Larry, he makes me
sick. Should be put down.

BRIAN: May I wash my hands?

JOAN: (*Turns and smiles.*) Certainly, my love. Through
there, but hurry. Get something inside you while it's hot.
(*She turns to a man who is passing plates of food through a
hatch to DOLORES and MICHELLE, who pass them around
the tables.*)
John! John! John! I'll brain you. I swear it.

VOICES: Is it dark out? Is it tomorrow? Arthur? Arthur!
Bloody bastard! What's on telly after dinner?
(*In a small room next to the dining room, BRIAN compulsively
washes his hands. Over and over again, he washes them, dries
them, and washes them again. BUZZ notices and realises that
the man is trapped with the water so he quietly creeps out of
the room, touches BRIAN and takes him into the dining room.
BRIAN watches the others eat.*)

BRIAN: Is there room?

DOLORES: (*Pushing other people along to make room for
BRIAN.*) I've got plenty of room for you.
(*BRIAN sits down, a bit confused.*)

BRIAN: I'm Brian Singleton.

DOLORES: I know. You told me.
(*A plate is placed before him. DOLORES shakes his hand
and won't let go.*)

BRIAN: Please. I'm hungry.
(*DOLORES lets his hand go and he starts to eat.*)

DOLORES: I can see… you're very hungry… Ooooooh…
aren't you?

LARRY: You're well in there, mate. Just you stay with us.
Take no notice of the others. They're all nutters. We're
on the slow mend as it were, but they're really off their
rockers. They should never have been let out. Don't trust

them. They're animals. Cannibals. You stay with us. You can be our friend. I'll put you right. You can trust me, but no one else.

(*DOLORES nearly chokes. LARRY points around the table to the various people.*)

That's Harold, he's harmless, mongol. Cretin. Stabbed his mother in the eye with a meat skewer. How long were you in that place?

(*BRIAN pretends not to hear.*)

Come on, we're all graduates from the nut house. How long were you there?

BRIAN: Twenty years.

LARRY: (*Whistles.*) Still, you're out now. Better late than never. Why were you in there so long?

BRIAN: But I didn't kill my mother.

(*Silence.*)

LARRY: Twenty years! That's a life sentence. Were you born with a screw loose? Or did it get shook off later?

BRIAN: Food's not bad.

DOLORES: Leave him alone, Larry.

LARRY: Shut up.

DOLORES: So's mine. Must be the weather.

LARRY: See him? Don't loan him money.

DOLORES: Don't loan no one money!

BRIAN: I haven't got any money to lend. But I'm very happy. I'm a guest now, a resident in a hotel. The authorities are very kind to send me here.

LARRY: Kind? Be blowed! It cost the powers-that-be a fortune to keep you in the looney bin and it costs them less than half that amount to keep you here in this little paradise hotel… It's economics. Statistics. (*He looks at BRIAN's plate.*) You had enough? You finished? Mind if I help myself?

DOLORES: He's a slow eater. Leave him alone.

MICHELLE: Him alone. Him alone.

BRIAN: It's alright. Help yourself.

(*LARRY does.*)

It's a very good idea, emptying the hospitals, sending us to the seaside for rehabilitation.

LARRY: You'll be rehabilitated in the cemetery, my old son. We're the sweepings under the carpet.

BRIAN: I don't understand.

LARRY: You will. And her, Milly, avoid her. She's got half her brain cut away. And that one's artistic.

DOLORES: Autistic.

LARRY: Anyway, she's dangerous.

DOLORES: Let him find out for himself.

MICHELLE: I was a good girl today.

BUZZ: (*Smiling and speaking apropos of nothing.*) Bastard... bastard... bastard... bastard...

VOICES: Bastard... bastard...

DOLORES: People get restless this time of evening before happy tabs.

LARRY: And that one over there, Charlie, he's got no balls. And Dennis next to him is only balls. That prune-faced one, Vera, she is being raped by every man twice a day. Brigid laughs all the time, and Bernadette cries all the time. Ali is a cretin. Primus is psychophrenic. I'm just an ordinary common or garden psychopath. (*Pointing to MICHELLE.*) She's not all here. (*Pointing to BUZZ.*) He's not all there, psychotic. (*To DOLORES.*) And she's a common or garden sex maniac.

DOLORES: Yeah, I'm a highly erogenous erotic. I need a gynachiatrist.

BRIAN: (*Innocently.*) I think I'm going to be very much at home here.

LARRY: That's about the lot. The rest you can forget. They're just sheep.

DOLORES: (*Sings.*) Poor little lambs, lost our way... ba... ba... ba...

JOAN: (*Off.*) Silence!

LARRY: (*Quietly to BRIAN.*) Oh, yeah, don't ever sit near stinkfinger.

BRIAN: Who?

LARRY: That filthy creature Reggie Costain. He's got crabs.

BRIAN: Pets?

(*They all laugh.*)

DOLORES: How he got them I'll never know. He's never had it in his life. (*To BRIAN.*) Roly poly and custard?

BRIAN: No thank you.

DOLORES: (*Sidling suggestively up to BRIAN.*) Hope you'll want afters another time. You've got lovely eyes, Brian. I hope you're not in the whip-it-in whip-it-out wipe-it brigade.

BRIAN: I'm going now. Long day.

(BRIAN leaves his food and LARRY takes it. BRIAN then approaches JOAN.)

Can I go upstairs and lie down? I've got a headache. I'm not used to travelling.

JOAN: Course, my little love. I'll show you your nice bed. It all must be so new, so confusing to you. So many new faces, new impressions. Come on, Brian, there's a good boy, up we go, up the wooden hill to Bedfordshire. And how long were you in that place? Twenty years, wasn't it?

(BRIAN nods.) I've got it in my records. Twenty years. That's a lifetime. Never mind, you're with us now.

(Out in the hall.)

BRIAN: May I take my coat?

JOAN: Certainly, certainly. Isn't it damp? Can't have you falling ill, now that you've started life all over again. *(Opens the door of a room.)* Here we are, you'll be very happy here.

What's up? Anything wrong, sweetheart?

(BRIAN perks up.)

Brian, you'll be very happy here. All my lovely boys are happy here. That's your bed, in the corner. Did you have your pills this morning before you left the hospital?

(BRIAN nods. She goes close and holds his chin, looks at him closely, smiling.)

You're phenothiazine, aren't you?

(He nods.)

You see? I remembered, off the top of my head. Don't worry. You won't have to manage without your happy tabs. We know everything about... we've got your papers. We've got it all organised. Have a rest. You'll have your evening tablet a little later. (*She is about to go but remembers something.*) Oh yes, Brian... I must have your supplementary pension book.

BRIAN: I thought I kept it.

JOAN: Of course not, darling. We don't want to lose it, do we? Give it to me. There's a good boy.

BRIAN: I want to write a letter.

JOAN: Of course, dear. To an auntie?

BRIAN: To my sister.

JOAN: (*A little surprised.*) Oh?

BRIAN: Where's the post box?

JOAN: Down the road, darling, you'll see it.

BRIAN: I want to buy a stamp. Where can I get a stamp?

JOAN: At the florist.

BRIAN: Florist?

JOAN: My pet! At the post office, of course. Where else?

BRIAN: Where's the post office? Can I go out later when I've written the letter? I must post the letter.

JOAN: I suggest you put your feet up and write the letter first. You've had a busy day. You can post it in the morning.

BRIAN: Yes. Thank you. Thanks.

(*She leaves the room. He is a bit lost for the moment. But then he perks up, puts on Glenn Miller and starts to unpack. He is still in his overcoat.*

He takes a photograph from his suitcase, puts it on the table, sits down, and writes a letter.)

(*Speaking as he writes.*) Dear Jeanette, You will be pleased to know that I have arrived safely in Margate. Yes, I am at the seaside. I feel so excited, like a five-year-old. I can hardly believe my luck. There's a wonderful funfair here called Dreamland. Maybe it will open when the weather's better. The new drugs are terrific, Jeanette. I no longer scream in the night, or want to smash people in the face, or wash my hands all the time. These pills really shield you and keep away the monsters. Thank God for modern science. I have been thrown a lifeline, Jeanette, and pulled out of the darkness. Incidentally, I gave up smoking a year ago. And crying. And I am going to try to cut back on these drugs. I'm almost normal. All my fondest love, from your optimistic brother, Brian. P.S. please send a recent photo. P.P.S. I just wanted you to know that at last everything seems to be going well for me. My life seems to have a bit of meaning. I feel I have a chance to pick up the pieces. At last I'm really happy.

(*Looks up and smiles. Then he starts to cry. Sobs across the table. Hugs the table. Cries and cries. Blackout.*

Next morning. The hall. MICHELLE and DOLORES are putting on their coats. BUZZ comes from the dining room, stuffing bread into his pockets. LARRY follows, opens the door, he shudders and shivers.)

LARRY: Christ, it's pissing down again. Look at those bloody dead streets; the cemetery's more inviting.

DOLORES: Margate out of season is like a whore without customers.

LARRY: You should know.

MICHELLE: Know. Know.

BUZZ: We can light a big fire today, Larry.

LARRY: Let's go to the crematorium and have a barbecue!

(*JOAN comes out of the kitchen.*)

JOAN: Come on then! What are you doing, standing by the window there like stuffed dummies? Out with you!

(*BUZZ backs away.*)

What's the matter?

BUZZ: I ain't got nothing in my pockets, honest I ain't got nothing in my pockets.

JOAN: What have you got in your pockets?

BUZZ: I ain't got no bread.

(*JOAN pulls his ear and delves into his pocket and pulls out some slices of bread.*)

JOAN: How dare you! People will think we starve you. You dare... you bloody well dare. Did you see him pinch this bread? Did you?

(*Nervously they shake their heads.*)

You dare lie, if I so much as catch you seeing something that you don't report to me, so help me, you'll be put out

on your ears. I'll wash my hands of you. Come on. Out!
God almighty, the things I have to put up with. You
devote your bloody life to the social services, you try to
help and nobody cares…
(*Then BRIAN comes.*)
Hello, darling… Are you all ready to go out then?
(*He nods.*)
Good boy. Wrap up warm. And don't forget your scarf.
(*She helps him wrap it round his neck.*) It's very cold today.
It's a real swine. Go with the others to the day centre,
darling. They'll show you the ropes… Bye…

BRIAN: (*Seeing the weather.*) Can't I…

JOAN: Brian, my love, it's nice to get out and get busy… to
learn how to get back into the world. There's my lovely
boy. And Mrs Killick will be ever so busy tidying up the
house and getting dinner ready. Bye bye for now, and as
the Yanks say, have a nice day! Toodle-oo!
(*Outside. The wind roars. They huddle in the doorway.*)

BRIAN: She's so nice. She's so very nice.

DOLORES: Yeah, like a fucking cobra.

BRIAN: I take as I find.

BUZZ: Which way, Larry? The long way or the short cut?

MICHELLE: Short cut, short cut…

DOLORES: What's the difference?

LARRY: She took your book, didn't she?

BRIAN: Book?

LARRY: Your allowance book. Like she took ours. It's your
personal property. She hasn't got any legal right to have
it. Why don't you ask for it back?

BRIAN: I can ask for it back any time.

LARRY: Yeah. Well, do it.

BRIAN: I'll do it.

LARRY: Well, do it then. What are you waiting for?
Christmas?

BRIAN: I shall do it. I'll do it now. (*Calling.*) Mrs Killick?

JOAN: Yes, Brian?

BRIAN: I would like my pension book back, please.

JOAN: No, dear.

BRIAN: I was told it was my property. I want it.

JOAN: Brian, you worry too much. We do the worrying here.

BRIAN: It's mine, I want it. (*Continues to mutter 'I want it.'*)

JOAN: Of course it's yours, dear, but we look after it for you, and we buy you all the little things you need to keep you nice and clean and happy. Toothpaste and choccies and we even give you fifty pence a week to buy ice cream and we do that throughout the year. So don't worry.

(*She has pushed him out and has gone. BRIAN recovers his composure.*)

BRIAN: I want to post a letter.

DOLORES: Who have you written to?

BRIAN: My sister. She's a famous actress.

DOLORES: So am I for five quid. To you, four pounds fifty. Come on, we can post it on the way to the centre. (*BRIAN follows the others, puts on his music.*)

LARRY: She won't abide that, you know. She can't abide personal music under her roof. She'll confiscate it.

BRIAN: I take as I find. I think for myself.

DOLORES: Which way's the wind blowing? (*Wets her finger and holds it up.*) Bloody hell, it's blowing all directions. Let's get to the day centre and out of this.

(*They arrive at the day centre and enter. The lights are bright, muzak plays, and it is warm. They sit together, rubbing hands, holding mugs. The PRIEST enters, smiling.*)

PRIEST: Hello, Buzz. Come for a singsong, have you? Good. Just the job. And nice to see such a happy face. God loves happy faces. He feels then that his hard work is rewarded. So let's all be happy! Are we all happy?

ALL: (*Shout.*) Yes.

DOLORES: Laugh and the laugh worlds with you, weep and you sleep alone. You cold, Brian? Ooch, your hands are like ice. (*Takes his hand.*)

PRIEST: Right. Now remember we're all friends here. I may be new, but already I feel like a trusted friend. So what's my name, everyone?

ALL: (*Shout.*) Reverend Robinson!

PRIEST: Right! But as I told you yesterday, please call me Mike. Right! Hello everyone.

ALL: (*Shout.*) Hello Mike!

PRIEST: That's better. So come on, folks, you're as young as you feel and as normal as the rest of us, so let it go with a swing. (*Calls to a pianist at the side.*) Cyril Rose, ladies and gentlemen, you know him well!
(*Everyone applauds. We do not see the pianist who is obviously taking a bow.*)
Cyril, take it away.
(*The piano starts to play.*)
So let it rip with a medley of sea and seaside songs. You all know this one. (*Starts to sing and conduct. Gradually they all join in.*) 'What shall we do with the drunken sailor? What shall we do with the drunken sailor...'

LARRY: (*Shouts.*) Bet you'd know what to do with a drunken sailor...
(*Everyone laughs, including the PRIEST. Now they all sing lustily.*)

ALL: Hooray, and up she rises...

DOLORES: (*Trying to touch BRIAN.*) 'Hooray, and up she rises... Hooray and up she rises, and three times on a Sunday!'

PRIEST: That was very good! And now – (*Sings.*) 'My bonny lies over the ocean, my bonny lies over the sea...'

ALL: 'I don't want to cause a commotion, so bring back my bonny to me. Bring back, bring back, oh bring back my bonny to me, to me...'
(*The singing continues. BRIAN is writing a letter in his mind. The lights focus on him and the rest of the scene goes dark. MICHELLE sits close and he looks at her. He might even be talking to her. She smiles sweetly.*)

BRIAN: Dear Jeanette, I've really settled in and already I've made some good friends. Today we are having a singsong in the day centre. A rather unusual priest is in charge. He has very modern methods and is very kind. He is a true Christian. Dear Jeanette, I have one great ambition. Guess what? Not to be stared at in the street. I think I might try and find a job. I must be good for something. Your loving brother, Brian.

(*He stops writing in his mind. The singsong returns.*)

ALL: 'All the nice girls love a sailor, All the nice girls love a tar...'

DOLORES: Brian! Join in! If you don't join in, it's no good.

PRIEST: And here's a really old favourite. Come on. This is the top of our pops.

(*He starts singing 'Red Sails in the Sunset'. Everyone joins in. BRIAN is really enjoying himself and smiles at DOLORES.*)

DOLORES: (*Quietly.*) You're cold. I'll warm you.

(*Takes his hand. He is petrified.*)

Try my central heating. (*She places his hand between her legs.*) And what have you got there between your legs?

BRIAN: Please...

DOLORES: (*Her other hand feeling him.*) Oh, my Gawd, it's magnificent. You've got a monster there, Brian, a sleeping giant.

(*BRIAN can stand no more. He gets up. The singsong stops.*)

BRIAN: 'Scuse me. Going for a walk.

PRIEST: Oh dear. We were all going to make baskets after this. Wouldn't you like to make a basket?

BRIAN: I am a basket. Goodbye.

(*Everyone laughs except the PRIEST. BRIAN leaves and walks onto the beach. Gulls screech. It is a rough day.*)

VOICES: (*Not unlike the gulls.*) Is it dark out, Arthur? Arthur! What's on telly? Go to the centre. Go to the centre. Is it tomorrow? Is it dark out?

(*BRIAN walks backwards and forwards like a caged animal. Then he sees two broken deckchairs. He assembles these until they represent a form of small shelter. He nestles within and plays Glenn Miller and looks perfectly content.*)

BRIAN: Ah, this is the life, this is the life... 'A jug of bread beneath the bough, A book of wine, a loaf of verse and thou...' (*Sings quietly, content.*) 'Oh, I do like to be beside... the seaside, Oh I do like to be beside the sea...

(*The wind howls, but BRIAN sings as if he actually means it.*)

I do like to stroll...'

(*Then he sees DOLORES standing above him.*)

DOLORES: Don't worry. Ain't gonna rape you!
(*BRIAN gets up, sees that the others are there. LARRY and BUZZ are lighting a fire.*)
(*Codding.*) 'Come on baby light my fire...' Light my fire, someone.

LARRY: No one's got the strength to keep you going.

DOLORES: You're right for once in your life. But I never knew how to utilise my energy. You see, Brian, I've always been too nice, too free and easy. If I was bad, I'd have made a fortune. I'd be married to someone in the House of Lords. Open legs are a gateway to society. But I did it all for love. I'm stupid. Would I be here otherwise? I don't even have a pot to piss in. I'm as daft as an arsehole.

BRIAN: (*Looking at MICHELLE.*) You alright, Michelle? She alright?
(*MICHELLE doesn't respond.*)

DOLORES: You'll get nothing out of her. No joy there. She's got nothing up there, and nothing down there. Not even two tits to rub together.

BRIAN: Please don't use such foul language. It's not nice.

DOLORES: Ain't he sweet?

LARRY: Come on, Dolores, tell us the story of your life.

BRIAN: (*Happy to divert her.*) Yes, please, that would be very nice.

BUZZ: Come on, Dolores.

DOLORES: Not again. Alright, twist my arm. (*Takes the stage.*)

LARRY: Here we go again.
(*DOLORES stands on a platform as if on a stage, others sit around like an audience.*)

DOLORES: Well, my downfall started in the front room. I was a beautiful child, prettiest girl in school, long golden hair, everyone stared at me in the street, but I wasn't a genius. I was terrible at maths. Well, my maths teacher offered to give me extra tuition in my house after school. He was ever so kind. My mother used to knock when she came into the room with tea and biscuits. One day she forgot to knock, she came straight in...

LARRY: And found him doing the knocking.

(*All laugh.*)

DOLORES: Anyway, they booted him out and three months later the piano needed tuning. The piano tuner called one day when my mother was out and he tuned me instead of the piano. After that I went round to his place where he tuned me twice nightly. I became overstrung. Me and my mum never stopped arguing at home. So, one day in the middle of the night, I crept downstairs and I left home for ever, and I started wandering and embarked on my life of endless depravity. I started wandering and I met so many hungry, sex-starved, depraved and lonely men.

(*LARRY lunges at her in fun, she pushes him away, laughing.*)
Poor things, I wanted to give them something, I was ever so sorry for them, but what did I have to give?

(*LARRY laughs, suggestively.*)
So there I was in this factory canteen, imagine thousands of workers sitting down about to eat lunch, there they were all shovelling toad-in-the-hole into their mouths and I think to myself, do I want to spend the rest of my life clearing plates? So I jump up onto this table and I shout 'Hey boys, who wants this for afters?' And I lift up my skirt (*Does so.*) and I pull down my drawers...

(*She does. BRIAN clenches his teeth in horror, but she has tights on under her knickers. She has been laughing, but we now realise she is crying, she is sobbing... still crying...*)
It was a sudden urge.

(*Gradually pulls herself together and pounces on BRIAN.*)

BRIAN: Please leave me alone.

DOLORES: (*Brighter now.*) It was a sudden urge, but it changed my life. From that day forth I became a fully fledged sexual maniac. Ooh, I feel ravenous. Come on boys, hold him down while he rapes me.

(*BUZZ and LARRY grab BRIAN; DOLORES is almost on top of him.*)

MICHELLE: (*Quietly.*) No.

(*Two yobbos enter: SPUNK and CRAPPER. Their transistor plays punk music. They look grotesque with clown-like paint*) *on their faces. They enjoy the scene, then they approach BUZZ and LARRY.)*

SPUNK: Look, a party! I love a party.

CRAPPER: *(Cod posh.)* And I say, a fire. Oh how dandy!

SPUNK: *(Camp.)* Light my fire, Crapper. *(Opens his arms in cod desire.)*

CRAPPER: With undying pleasure, Spunk.

(They embrace, pretending to kiss and make love. BUZZ laughs.)

Who you laughing at? You fucking pig, you spastic. I'll smash your face in. Whole town's full of you creeps.

SPUNK: You shitting idiots, you shitcunts.

(They go towards LARRY.)

And clock this loon! And her! They lower the tone, don't they, Crapper?

CRAPPER: Yers, Spunk, there I agree. They give this town a bad name.

BUZZ: More out than in, more out than in.

SPUNK: What did you say?

BRIAN: He didn't say anything.

CRAPPER: *(Looking at BRIAN.)* The whole rotten town is rotten with madmen and you look like the king of the loons, don't you agree?

BRIAN: If you say so.

SPUNK: I think they're a danger to public health, don't you, Crapper?

CRAPPER: Yer. *(He sees MICHELLE.)* Hello, darlin'.

(MICHELLE smiles.)

DOLORES: You leave her alone. Git.

SPUNK: Ooh, at least the birds have got spirit.

(SPUNK and CRAPPER start kicking the fire and laughing.)

BUZZ: *(Attacking them as LARRY cringes away.)* You leave my flames alone.

(They start hitting BUZZ and BRIAN goes to his defence.)

SPUNK: *(Turning on BRIAN.)* Come on, Crapper, let's kill the bastard.

(But they suddenly notice BRIAN's violence. CRAPPER still smiles but doesn't seem so keen to attack.)

Come on, Crapper! What you waiting for?

CRAPPER: Nutcase! Nutcase! Spastic!

(*BUZZ goes berserk, hitting out, flailing around, hammering his fists at the laughing SPUNK and CRAPPER.*)

BUZZ: Larry! Larry!

(*As SPUNK and CRAPPER close in, LARRY cringes away. DOLORES comes to the boys' assistance and BRIAN moves in. At first he clenches his teeth as if trying to stop himself, then he grabs SPUNK. The boy is rendered powerless by BRIAN's terrible fury. CRAPPER freezes.*)

BRIAN: (*Quietly.*) If you don't leave us alone, I'll kill you.

(*Everything goes quiet.*)

SPUNK: (*Pleads.*) Please let me go, mister.

(*BRIAN releases him.*)

CRAPPER: Come on, Spunk, let's blow, it might be catching.

SPUNK: Yer, bloody loons. Shitting nuts. (*Then to MICHELLE.*) Bye, darlin'.

(*They run off laughing. LARRY comes out of his hole and with quixotic bravado runs a small way after them.*)

LARRY: Come back and fight, you cowards. We got them on the run, didn't we? Let's go after them. Come on.

DOLORES: Bloody coward.

MICHELLE: Coward.

LARRY: Yer, bloody cowards.

DOLORES: I meant you.

BUZZ: More out than in, more out than in.

(*BRIAN is laughing. Lightning. Thunder. Pouring rain.*)

DOLORES: Brian. What's the matter? Why you so happy?

BRIAN: You don't understand. I won. I didn't hit them. I didn't go too far. I could have really hurt them and I didn't. Don't you see? I really won.

DOLORES: Yes. And now you deserve your reward. Come on, Brian. Lie down. Come on, lie down with me… Come on, Brian, it's nice, you'll like it. Touch me. Touch me.

BRIAN: No.

DOLORES: Why not?

BRIAN: I've got to phone my sister. (*He runs away.*)

(*DOLORES suddenly looks like an old woman.*)

DOLORES: Oh, Christ!

(*The scene darkens. Night. The lounge at the Colonnade Hotel. Various VOICES call from the other rooms. Someone keeps sighing. Someone is quietly crying. Everyone is agitated.*)

VOICES: Oh dear, oh dear…

(*These VOICES continue intermittently through this scene.*)

Oh dear… Oh dear, oh dear, oh dear…

DOLORES: Well, go to Woolworths then.

VOICE: Help, help, help!

LARRY: Arthur? Arthur!

BUZZ: Bastard! Bastard!

VOICE: What's on telly? Nothing good on telly. Go to Woolworths then. Go to Woolworths, go to Woolworths, go to Woolworths then…

MICHELLE: Go to the centre. Go to the centre.

DOLORES: Don't worry, darling. No point feeling low. You'll never get out of life alive.

BRIAN: Not worried. Look at them. (*Refers to the people we cannot see who are apparently sitting watching TV.*) Don't they do anything else?

VOICE: Is it dark out? Is it night? Going to the centre. What's on telly? Nothing good on telly.

BRIAN: For three days that TV screen's been slipping. Won't someone fix it?

VOICES: Go to Woolworths then. Go to Woolworths. Arthur! Arthur!

DOLORES: Well, fix it then.

VOICE: Bastard! Bastard!

MICHELLE: Fix it. Fix it.

BRIAN: What time is it?

DOLORES: Don't despair. Almost time for the chemical cosh.

BRIAN: Thank God. Get restless about now. Need it. But going to cut down. I promised. I promised. (*Hits the walls.*) Hurt myself. (*Laughs terribly.*) Chemical leucotomy they call it.

DOLORES: Lew who?

BRIAN: Supposedly reversible. (*Paces again.*) What time is it? Can't get into life. It's all this cotton wool in the brain. If only I could get it out.

DOLORES: Yes, please.

BRIAN: Sex! Sex! Sex! That's all you know! (*He holds her, impassioned.*) Dolores, please! I've got to improve myself. I mustn't vegetate.

LARRY: Shut up! Shut up! It was quiet here till you came.

BRIAN: (*Glowers at him.*) Sorry. No offence. (*Sits at the table.*) Yes, yes. Write a letter.

LARRY: You never seem to get one back.

BUZZ: He does. (*To LARRY.*) Shut up, you fart.

MICHELLE: My mummy! My mummy, she said… (*She forgets.*)

(*VOICES continue droning, sighing, laughing. Everything darkens. BRIAN starts to write.*)

BRIAN: (*Talking to MICHELLE.*) I can't blame her for her total silence. I know I've been a terrible disappointment to Jeanette. I can understand why she ignores me. For the past twenty years I must have been a terrible liability. Twenty years? Was it twenty years?

(*MICHELLE, over-attentive to his words, nods her head eagerly but sometimes shakes her head sadly.*)

Moments drag, but years flash by. It's been a wasted lifetime. But that's all in the past. As I told you, they are opening up the mental hospitals, they don't need straight-jackets any longer. What with modern drugs, I am in the process of being de-institutionalised, of coming back from the living dead. The winter gets into my bones, I long for summer when the funfair opens. Pray God I can make it and we can be reunited, the food is quite good here, plain, no nonsense. I am not too depressed. Rehabilitation is not easy.

LARRY: Rehabilitation!

(*He laughs uproariously. The others join in.*
JOAN and JOHN enter the lounge. BRIAN stops writing.)

JOAN: Come on, poppets. Happy tabs! Come on! Anyone would think you'd be only too happy to get your sweet dreams. Come on! Look alive.

(*All queue up.*)

Wipe your nose, there's a good girl. And just look at this lump. I'll chuck you out for the dustman.

DOLORES: What's up?

BRIAN: Nothing.

DOLORES: Come on. Medicine.

BRIAN: Don't need it. (*He is shaking.*) Do you know, Dolores? It's occurred to me. Only three sorts of people in this world, the pre-mad, the mad and the post-mad. We're post-mad.

DOLORES: Four types, there's also the sex-mad. Come on.

JOAN: Come on, come on then. (*Talks as if they are babies.*) Stick out your tongue…

(*JOHN reads case notes and hands her tablets. JOAN administers to the long queue of shuffling people.*)

Come on. Don't want any of your stupid tricks. No good you trying to save all those pills for a rainy day 'cause that rainy day is here and now.

(*VOICES now, agitated before medicine.*)

That's right, Dolores. Good girl. There we are. That's the way. All the way down.

(*BRIAN has not joined the queue.*)

(*Softly cajoling.*) Brian? Brian…

BRIAN: No. No. No. No. No. No. No! No!

JOAN: There's my lovely little chap. There's my poppet. Come and get your happy tab.

BRIAN: (*Quietly.*) Mrs Killick. I have decided that I don't want drugs.

JOAN: Come now, there's a good boy.

BRIAN: I have decided to cut back. I'm… I'm not like the others. I am being rehabilitated. That's why I am here. I'm normal now.

JOAN: Course you are.

BRIAN: I'm no longer a mental case, remember?

JOAN: (*Soothingly.*) Brian, listen. We know what is best for you. We have your history here. We know that if you don't have your drugs regularly, twice a day, you become very upset. And we don't want that, do we, my love? Come on, there's a good boy.

BRIAN: (*Rigid. Angry.*) I am not upset. I am not upset. I don't want to hit you. I don't want to hit you. I am not upset and I don't want to hit you. I am cutting down on my

drugs. I am not… going… I am not… going… not
going… I am cutting… not hitting… not going to smash…

JOAN: Yes, yes, you'll be alright.

BRIAN: Please Mrs Killick, just let me try…

JOHN: (*Reading notes.*) Ah yes, Brian… You're phenothiazine,
aren't you?

LARRY: (*To DOLORES.*) That explains it… He's a pheno…
those pheno's are the worst. They're dangerous. They can
break out at any moment.

(*BRIAN stands with his lips clenched tight.*)

JOAN: (*With the tablet and a glass of water placed to BRIAN's
lips.*) There's a good boy.

BRIAN: (*Through clenched lips.*) No… No…

JOAN: There's a love… open your mouth… Come on
Brian, there's a good boy.

(*BRIAN opens his mouth and then swallows.*)

BRIAN: (*Happily.*) All gone.

(*Everyone is extremely relieved. JOAN ruffles his hair.*)

JOAN: Right, beddybyes, everyone. No more dawdling.
Night, night. Sleep tight. Mind the bugs don't bite.

LARRY: (*To BRIAN.*) You see, mate, you're getting wise.
It's easier to do things their way. 'Cause if you're thrown
out and you're not re-certified, you get a reputation as
a trouble-maker. No one will take you on. These hotel
owners have got their own tribal drums. Beware Brian
Singleton… don't take him… If you make trouble here
you'll end up on the rubbish heap. (*Taps his head.*) It pays
to have a screw loose. It gets you off the hook. Oh well,
time for bed.

MICHELLE: Brian?

(*BRIAN goes to her. She smiles kindly. He gently touches
her face.*)

BRIAN: I am definitely giving up drugs. Tomorrow. We're
all zombies. But not yours truly. Tomorrow, you'll see.
I am determined to do something with my life. That's
why they let me out. My mind is made up… No more
chemical coshes for me. You'll see. Made up my mind.
And I can do it, Jeanette, I know I can. And I will not
resort to violence. And smash people over the skull with

a poker. I never killed my mother. I swear it. I miss you, Jeanette. Without you, I'd cut my throat with a bread knife. I'm going to wash now and then I'm off to bed. Night, night.

(*Goes to wash but he is trapped in washing. He washes obsessively. The PRIEST enters and sits on BUZZ's bed. They joke together. Then the PRIEST talks to LARRY who touches him for a fag. The PRIEST goes round and talks to everyone in the cramped room. Then he sees BRIAN.*)

BRIAN: Help me...

PRIEST: Of course I will, my son.

BRIAN: Tell Mrs Killick. (*Still compulsively washing his hands.*) Please tell her I must give up these drugs. Convince her. Help me... Help me... I can't think. Can't plan ahead. Can't remember.

PRIEST: You must rest, Brian.

BRIAN: (*Appealing to PRIEST.*) I'm rehabilitated. That's why I'm here. I mustn't take the drugs. It's a chemical cosh. Please help me, please.

PRIEST: If you promise to go to bed.

BRIAN: But I'm washing first.

PRIEST: Yes, and the leper shall be washed clean.

BRIAN: Can the leper change his spots?

PRIEST: A good sleep will do you good.

BRIAN: Thank you, Reverend... Thank you, Mike.

LARRY: No priest ever came near us at bedtime before. Except you. Very nice.

PRIEST: I've come to lead you all in a goodnight singsong.

MICHELLE: Singsong?

PRIEST: Yes. I do not only believe in conventional prayer to reach God. I believe that singing is another form of prayer, so let's all have a singsong before we sleep.

BRIAN: (*Sings to himself like a child.*) 'Now the day is over, night is drawing nigh, shadows of the evening steal across the sky...'

PRIEST: Why not something more rousing? God can be a little hard of hearing these days. Let's sing a rousing hymn!

BRIAN: Hear, hear!

PRIEST: Let's sing 'To be a pilgrim.' (*Sings and they all join in.*)

ALL: (*Lustily.*) 'He who would valiant be 'gainst all disaster, let him in constancy follow the Master. There's no discouragement shall make him once relent, His first avowed intent to be a pilgrim.'

PRIEST: Bravo! (*Claps.*) Jolly good. And now goodnight to you all. And God bless you all. Come on, ladies, before Mrs Killick comes.

MICHELLE: (*Goes off.*) To be a pilgrim. To be a pilgrim… To be a good girl… Bye bye, Brian.

DOLORES: Night, Brian. And don't be naughty in the night and sleepwalk 'cause I won't know how to defend myself. (*She goes. Darkness. BRIAN puts cassette on, quietly. The song is 'At Last'.*)

LARRY: Night.

(*Men cough and snore.*)

BRIAN: Night.

LARRY: Night, Buzz.

(*No reply.*)

I said 'night, Buzz.'

(*No reply.*)

I said 'goodnight, Buzz.' Buzz? Buzz?

BRIAN: Goodnight, Larry. Goodnight, Buzz.

LARRY: He won't reply. He's far too busy.

BRIAN: Busy?

LARRY: Course. Bashing the old bishop.

BRIAN: I wouldn't know.

LARRY: Come off it, Brian. What about them circles under your eyes? You've got wanker's doom. You're a wanker!

BRIAN: Goodnight.

LARRY: You see, Buzz, everyone does it… You carry on, my old son. You pull it and enjoy it.

BUZZ: (*Quietly.*) One day, Larry, I'm going to fry your eyeballs and eat them.

LARRY: Might be better than the food you get here. Anyway if you killed me you'd be doing me a favour. Night.

BRIAN: Night. Night. Night, one and all. (*Quietly.*) Dear Jeanette, goodnight.

End of Act One.

ACT TWO

Bedrooms. Morning. Everyone in bed. A bell goes. Everyone jumps out of bed. They all jump out too fast.

BRIAN remains in bed. He croons quietly, thinking he's Bing Crosby.

LARRY: She'll be up any moment.

BRIAN: I'm staying in bed today.

(LARRY and BUZZ laugh.)

LARRY: Don't say I didn't warn you.

(JOAN comes in. Everyone cringes away. She smiles as she quietly approaches BRIAN's bed. BRIAN is happy. Then she pulls back the blankets. He has his shoes on, plus his overcoat over his pyjamas.)

JOAN: How dare you? How dare you defy me? Down! Down!

(The others quickly go and queue downstairs. JOAN turns again to BRIAN who is cowering on the bed.)

You dare, you bloody well dare...

BRIAN: Please! I'm sorry. I didn't know the rules.

JOAN: Up! Out! Down! You snivelling, stinking creature. Up! Get up I say! You oaf, you sleep in your shoes again and I'll ram them down your throat!

BRIAN: Sorry. Sorry. Sorry. Sorry.

JOAN: *(Noticing his cassette.)* What's this? *(She switches it on and Glenn Miller plays.)* So you're the one who's responsible for that racket. I'll confiscate that for a start.

BRIAN: It's mine! *(He goes towards her with his fists clenched.)* I want it, it's mine.

JOAN: *(Screaming.)* Don't you touch me! Don't you raise your hands to me!

(JOHN comes running in.)

BRIAN: Sorry. Sorry!

JOAN: *(Seeing JOHN.)* Right! Did you see that? That's it. He's out on his ear.

BRIAN: Please! Give me a chance. I'm going to look for a job today.

JOAN: *(Her mood changes. She starts to laugh.)* What? *(To JOHN.)* Did you hear that? Did you ever hear such a funny joke in your life? (*To BRIAN.*) Don't you understand? You're hopeless, useless. Do you honestly think that you are of any value to anyone? It's about time you came down to earth. (*She turns to JOHN.*) He looks like a troublemaker. I knew it when I first clapped eyes on him.

JOHN: Listen, Joanie. I think you're right. You're always right. But we'd better be careful. You know as well as I do that the local press are just waiting for an opportunity to have a go at us. He's not like the others. I have a funny feeling he could spell trouble.

JOAN: You're right. I didn't want to take him in the first place. I should have trusted my instincts. (*To BRIAN.*) Right! Out of the goodness of my heart I'm going to give you another chance. But step out of line just once more and that's it! Now, downstairs, and get into line. And not another word out of you! (*Sweeps out.*)

JOHN: You're bloody daft, you know.

BRIAN: Wouldn't be here if I wasn't.

JOHN: You can't win. Just keep on the good side of her.

BRIAN: Thank you, Mr Killick. You're a gentleman.

(*There is a bond of sympathy between them. Downstairs, they are all queuing for pills.*)

BRIAN: (*The queue moves slowly. He talks to himself.*) Dear Jeanette. Things are not going very well for me at the moment. Incidentally, did I ever hit you as a child? If so, it would explain why you don't answer my letters.
I never killed Mother, you know. I'm sure, even though most of my childhood I wasn't all there. If I ever hit you I apologise. You see, somewhere, somewhere, somewhere, somewhere in my head I can hear you screaming.
I think, I think, I think, I think, I think I was trying to bite off your nose. Please reply by return of post and tell me this is not true. I'm going to look for a job today. Maybe I'll leave Margate and try my luck elsewhere. Trouble is, wherever I go I take my head with me.
I'll decide tomorrow. Pills now. Happy tabs. Happy tabs. Close down. Goodbye then, goodbye then. Goodbye.

Goodbye. Now about to get my pills but I am going to try to manage without, without, without. All my love, Brian.

(*He gets his tablet. JOAN is distracted so he only pretends to swallow it. He slips the pill into his shoe. She gives him water.*)

All gone.

DOLORES: It's pissing out. Pissing, pissing, pissing.

LARRY: It's God pissing on the world.

BRIAN: Can't blame him.

LARRY: He's pissing to fill up the ocean.

BRIAN: I like the ocean.

DOLORES: It's dirty dishwater.

LARRY: It's only waiting, you know. One of these days the sea will flood right over us, and God will come and pull the chain and we'll all go anti-clockwise down the plughole.

MICHELLE: (*Dipping into her plate.*) Porridge.

LARRY: Yeah, a life sentence.

BUZZ: I like storms at sea. Plenty of driftwood.

DOLORES: But no shipwrecked mariners.

MICHELLE: Porridge! Porridge.

DOLORES: It's not. It's sick.

LARRY: It's not sick. It's vomit.

BRIAN: I think the human race is a very nice branch of evolution. I'm happy. I'm really happy.

MICHELLE: Happy porridge! (*Starts splashing.*)

DOLORES: (*Restraining her.*) Why you so happy this morning?

BRIAN: I'm not going to the day centre with you lot.

LARRY: What you gonna do then?

BRIAN: Look for a job.

(*LARRY splutters in his tea. Everyone laughs. BRIAN is not perturbed.*)

LARRY: Face facts. You're useless. You'd stand a better chance if you were a criminal. At least in prison you can get trained for something.

BRIAN: I'm different. I'm me. I'm not going to lay down and die. (*Goes off singing.*)

(*Everyone laughs and laughs.*
On the beach. It is dark and very stormy.)

DOLORES: (*Reading to MICHELLE from a magazine.*)
'Dear Aunt Veronica, my boyfriend brought me a cup
of instant coffee and in return wanted my whole body.
What shall I do? Dear Sharon, It depends on the blend.'
(*She laughs.*) Listen to this one…

LARRY: (*Falling over and laughing.*) This is how I found the
golden rivet…

BUZZ: Where is it now, Larry?

LARRY: Oh, someone unscrewed it, Buzz, and my arse
dropped off.
(*Silence: he starts to sing 'Sleepy Lagoon'. BRIAN enters.*)

BRIAN: (*Announces.*) I'm going to drown myself.

MICHELLE: Bye, bye, Brian.
(*BRIAN walks into the sea.*)

BUZZ: Brian! Brian! It's deep out there. (*Calling.*) Dolores!
Did you see him? Brian's gone into the water.

DOLORES: What? Where?

MICHELLE: Brian. Bye bye, Brian.

DOLORES: BRIAN! (*Runs towards BRIAN.*)

BRIAN: And the leopard shall be cleansed. Help! Help!
Help! Help me! Help me, someone! I can't swim. Can't
swim. Can't swim. Going down. (*Choking, going down.
Coming up again, again and again.*) Jeanette! Help… me…

DOLORES: Hold on, Brian. Hold on! (*Hoicks up her skirts.*)
I'm coming.
(*She reaches him in the sea and grabs him and struggles and
swims around with him. Pulls him out, and they lie exhausted
next to each other.*)
You alright?
(*No reply.*)
You dead?
(*No reply.*)
Do you need the kiss of life?
(*He quickly jumps up.*)

BRIAN: Thanks, you saved my life.

DOLORES: (*Laughs.*) How can I save you when I can't even
swim myself? You should take your drugs like everyone

else and be a good boy. (*She starts shivering.*) Guess what
I fancy?

BRIAN: A hot drink. I could do with a cup of tea.

DOLORES: Remember Burt Lancaster and Deborah Kerr
in that film, From Here to Maternity? The way they did
it on the seashore, in the waves? Burt, I'm all yours.

BRIAN: Or a cup of cocoa...

DOLORES: Oh, alright, virgin. Here, have a drop
of whisky.

BRIAN: Where did you get the money?

DOLORES: I print it between my legs, don't I?

BUZZ: Here, Larry, want some of this?

LARRY: You know I never touch the stuff and you shouldn't
neither.

(*BUZZ gives the bottle to MICHELLE.*)

LARRY: Don't give her any! Oh, Christ.

(*BRIAN ritualistically washes his hands in the sea.*)

DOLORES: You don't have to wash your hands all the time,
you know.

BRIAN: I do, I wash my hands, I wash my hands, I wash
my hands because... I wash my hands because I have to.
Don't want to talk about it.

DOLORES: (*She sings 'Goodbye, Yellow Brick Road'.*) Oh,
Elton, Elton, if you only made love to me you'd turn
normal. Don't worry, Brian, just accept that nothing
is going to change. It's worse if you actually believe
all that crap that the social services put out about
reha-bloody-bilitation!

BRIAN: I want to go back to Clayton. It was home. It's
dangerous out here.

DOLORES: What went wrong with us? What did we do to
deserve this?

BRIAN: I don't know. I never killed my mother.

DOLORES: I mean... Life's difficult enough even when
you've got all your faculties. Ain't you got any family?
'Spect you're like me.

BRIAN: (*Defensively.*) I've got my sister.

DOLORES: She doesn't seem to be concerned about you.

BRIAN: She's very busy.

DOLORES: Sorry. No one else?

BRIAN: My mother looked after me until I was twenty. I was like lost property. In Harrow-on-the-Hill. All my childhood I wasn't really there. I was locked up in my head. But my mother was there until she died. I took her breakfast in bed every morning. Apparently when they found me she was dead. She had been dead a week. There were seven lots of breakfast on the eiderdown in front of her. I can remember that. They came into the room with handkerchiefs pressed to their noses, and they tore me away from her. Then they drove me away. Far, far away. They were very kind to me at first. But then they let me alone, forgot about me. I didn't bother them, they didn't bother me. They were so busy. So many people were going mad all the time.

DOLORES: And that was twenty years ago? When you went in?

(*BRIAN nods.*)

And you were twenty years there in Clayton?

BRIAN: Twenty years next February. February the sixth.

DOLORES: That's a long time, Brian. Never mind, you're out now. Smile then. Smile for me.

(*He does.*)

Good boy. Always keep your pecker up.

(*He laughs.*)

Dirty so-and-so. Cheers!

(*They drink and she starts to sing 'Red Sails in the Sunset', holding her hands open as if she were on a stage. They all start singing drunkenly, BRIAN changes the song to 'Sunny Side of the Street'. They all dance around until they reach the hotel. MICHELLE, LARRY and BUZZ quietly go to back room, but DOLORES and BRIAN sing noisily in the hall.*)

DOLORES: Sssssh! We're here! She'll serve up your gizzard for supper! (*Holding her hand between her legs like a little girl.*) 'Scuse me, darling, I must go where no one can go for me.

JOHN: (*Going to BRIAN.*) Hide, Brian, hide! (*Pushes BRIAN down under a table.*) If she catches you pissed, that's it! (*BRIAN crouches under the table when JOAN comes in. JOHN quickly opens his arms and starts to sing, as if serenading his wife.*)

JOAN: You fool! Blithering idiot! Imbecile! What an example! What can I do with this man? It's finished. I can't take any more. Fool! Twit! Christ, I'll kill you! I've had enough. Just about enough! Look at him! Look at the big man! Look at my husband! What a noble specimen! You make me puke.
(*Everything goes quiet. She is at the end of her tether.*)

LARRY: Please, Mrs Killick. Just wanted to say that… that… Brian's gone out. He just went out… He just left… just before… Honest… I'm not lying.

JOAN: (*Tearfully.*) Right! That's it! That is it! Tomorrow Mr Brian Singleton is out on his ear. That's all we needed, a lunatic like him on the loose at night in Margate. He'll rape someone or worse and we'll carry the can! Go out and get him. Go and find him. What the bloody hell you waiting for? Go! Go!

JOHN: Joanie! It's pointless! It's useless!

JOAN: Find the bloody fool. Just go and find him.
(*JOHN doesn't move. JOAN leaves.*
BRIAN is on the beach, looking up at the sky.)

BRIAN: Universe. So vast. So perfect. Why couldn't I be born normal? Small thing like me? Poor Mr Killick, even being normal is hard enough. Only got one prayer, just one little prayer. Surely it can be granted. Please don't let me be stared at in the street. It's scary, the sky, so many stars, but not so scary as Madgate. (*Sings quietly.*) 'No goblins nor foul fiend shall daunt his spirit. He knows he at the end will life inherit. Though fancies flee away, he'll fear not what men say, He'll labour night and day to be a pilgrim.' (*Shivers.*) Cold! Afraid! Alone! No. No self pity. Brian boy, no one wants your sorrow. If you're lucky you'll enjoy all that jam tomorrow, but I'd love some jam tonight. Some marmalade would put me right. Then I would fight with all my might, to be… just normal. (*Punches the sand.*) A girl! Yes, a girl would put me right.

A normal girl who wouldn't care what I am but only what I could be. Jeanette, if only I could perfect my dancing. (*He starts singing a waltz and dancing to it. In the background we hear the others playing bingo at the day centre. LARRY wins and they come onto the beach. They stand silently and watch BRIAN dancing. Suddenly he sees them. Hops around.*)

BRIAN: (*Embarrassed.*) I trod on a nail.

(*All enter.*)

BUZZ: Hello.

BRIAN: Hello, Buzz.

BUZZ: How are you?

BRIAN: I'm fine. How are you?

BUZZ: I'm fine. Nice weather for this time of the year.

BRIAN: I'm not so sure.

BUZZ: You coming home?

BRIAN: No. Never.

BUZZ: Oh, goodbye then. He doesn't want to come home.

DOLORES: You should come back, Brian, and have your happy tab.

BRIAN: No. I'm not coming with you.

DOLORES: Brian, you've got to learn to conform, otherwise you're finished.

BRIAN: No. I'm not coming back and that's that. I've made up my mind.

DOLORES: Come on, Larry, we've got to take him back.

LARRY: What's the point, she'll be throwing him out in the morning anyway.

BRIAN: I'm never going back. I'm only going forward. I'm going forward to the past. I've thought it all out. I'm going to Kent.

BUZZ: We're in Kent.

BRIAN: No, this is a different Kent, this is. This one's buried under the motorway. My mother and all her family used to go hop-picking there. Gran. Grandad. Auntie Sophie. Mr and Mrs Norton. Stan and Mercy Whitcomb...

DOLORES: We used to go on holiday with my Auntie Rose when I was a kid. I had pigtails. That was before my mother met my uncle... I won't tell you what he did...

BRIAN: When the fields of hops were ready, everyone just packed up and the East End became empty. We poured down there in our thousands. For three glorious weeks we were there in Kent. It was like a carnival. That's what I'm going back to.

DOLORES: I wish I could go back to the past.

BRIAN: It's a different planet. People were nicer. My parents. People were human. Pre-plastic. Pre-detergent. Pre-neurotic mankind.

LARRY: That was when beer was beer and tasted like the smell of the fields.

BRIAN: Not the muck they sell now but golden ale. Ale that doesn't exist any more. Ale they banished because people loved it too much. 'Here we go hopping down in Kent.' It's been locked in my brain all these years. (*Sings.*) 'Here we go a-hopping… A-hopping down in Kent…'

BUZZ: We're in Kent.

MICHELLE/BUZZ: 'Here we go…' (*They continue singing.*)

BRIAN: That's where I'm going. You can go back to Mrs Killick if you like but I'm going to join an endless army of happy laughing people singing songs round the camp fire, joking and playing under a starry sky.

BUZZ: Can I come, Brian? I want to go hopping.

BRIAN: Yes, that's it. Come with me, all of you. You don't need Mrs Killick there, or happy tabs or anything. It's a golden opportunity to get away from godforsaken Margate.

DOLORES: I'm not sure.

BRIAN: Please, Dolores, you're spoiling everything. Unhappiness hasn't been invented yet. No violence. Just the glorious smell of hops and fields of gold.

DOLORES: How can we get there?

BRIAN: We'll march. We'll march 'cause we're not dead yet. (*He starts quietly singing 'To be a Pilgrim'. He inspires them and gradually they join in. Triumphant they begin to march away. During their song they shout.*) Goodbye, Mad-gate.

BUZZ: Goodbye, Mrs Killick.

MICHELLE: Bye bye, Margate.

LARRY: Goodbye, world.

(*They march on.*)

BRIAN: (*Points.*) Canterbury! Turn left. We're going right, for this is the way. Onward! Onward! Into the valley of England! Onward to freedom. Onward for sanity, happiness, England, St. Michael and the British Home Stores.

LARRY: Can't go on.

BRIAN: Onward!

LARRY: Let me die here.

BRIAN: Onward! Onward! (*He tries to rouse them. Sings.*) 'There's no discouragement shall make him once relent…' Come on, Dolores. 'His first avowed intent to be a pilgrim…'

DOLORES: Where are we?

BRIAN: We're on our way to Chapman's farm.

DOLORES: Why Chapman's farm?

BRIAN: That's the one she used to go to. It's famous. It's between Canterbury and Faversham on the A2.

LARRY: You said it was between Canterbury and Charing. We're lost.

MICHELLE: We're lost. We're lost. We're lost.

BRIAN: I know exactly where we are. If you breathe in you can smell the hops.

(*They all sniff.*)

And when we get there, we'll know at once. There are two oasthouses silhouetted against the sky and then the fields and fields of hops. Tall rows of silent warriors. Giant sentries. (*Sings.*) 'Here we go looby loo…' Come on, we want to get there before dark. 'Here we go looby lie…'

LARRY: Not moving.

BRIAN: Alright, let's have a rest.

DOLORES: I'm going to bed. Anyone coming to bed?

BRIAN: (*Relishing the view.*) Nature. The priest is in the church and God is in the fields.

LARRY: I'm starving. Listen to my stomach. It's revolting.

DOLORES: Telling me.

BUZZ: Wait. Wait! (*He can hear something.*) I'll be back in a minute. (*Quickly pulls his coat over his head.*)

LARRY: (*Seeing letters stuck out of BRIAN's pocket.*) What's this? Letters? Dirty letters. Who to, Brian? Hey, listen to this... Dear Jeanette... Oooohh...

BRIAN: (*Springs and snatches the letters back. He talks quietly.*) If you ever do that again, I'll kill you.

(*LARRY understands.*)

I trust you, Michelle, because you don't talk to anyone.

(*MICHELLE nods.*)

Never tell a friend a secret because your friend has a friend.

(*MICHELLE nods.*)

You see, Michelle, I am reconstructing my life. The way I see it, Margate is in the past... we'll earn a small fortune gathering hops. Yes?

(*MICHELLE happily nods.*)

Then I'm going to Southampton to find my sister. I'll have enough money to support myself so I shan't be a burden on her. And guess what? I might take Buzz with me, because he's my best friend. I'm sure my sister won't mind. I'd like to take you as well but I think Dolores would miss you, wouldn't she.

(*MICHELLE nods.*)

Do you mind?

(*MICHELLE nods, smiling, not really understanding his words.*)

Do you love me?

(*MICHELLE nods.*)

Do you hate me?

(*MICHELLE nods.*)

I really think that Buzz is a nice person don't you? He is so very sweet and innocent. I think my sister will adore him. The three of us will have great times together.

(*BUZZ approaches.*)

I was saying, Buzz, I've written to my sister about you, so it's all arranged. After we've made enough money hopping, you're coming to Southampton with me.

BUZZ: Am I?

BRIAN: You'll love it. We can stand on the dockside and watch the liners slipping in and out, travelling to the other side of the world. And after we've settled in with

my sister and made a base, we'll get a job on the QE2 as
deck stewards. We'll go to New York and look at the
Statue of Liberty. What do you think, Buzz?

BUZZ: I'm the king of the castle, you're a dirty rascal.

BRIAN: (*Hears a lorry.*) Quick! Transport! We could do with
a lift.

DOLORES: Hold on! This is my speciality! Everyone hide.
Back in the hedge. Leave it to me.
(*They all hide and she goes to the centre of the road, lifts her
skirt, and pulls down her knickers. BRIAN hides his eyes.
The lorry screeches to a stop.*)
Right. Everyone in the back. I'm doing a deal in the
front with the driver.
(*They rush to the lorry and it starts. Laughter in the darkness.
A journey. They sing in darkness.*)

ALL: 'There was butter, butter, scraped up from the gutter
in the stores, in the stores. There was butter, butter,
scraped up from the gutter in the quartermaster's stores.
My eyes are dim I cannot see, I have not got my specs
with me…'

DOLORES: (*Off.*) Oh… naughty boy. Ooh naughty boy.
Yes. Yes. Yes. Yes, yes, yes, oh yes.

BRIAN: Dear Jeanette. Dear Jeanette. Here we are on our
way. We were all long-term prisoners, zombies of the
world. We have nothing to lose, because we have nothing.
We are nothing. Long-term prisoners and the sentence was
life without hope, but all that's changed. We are pilgrims
on the road to life and we won't be stared at any more.
'I'll give you one o, green grow the rushes o.'
(*The lorry stops. They emerge into a desolate landscape. But
for the moment they are still happy.*)

DOLORES: (*Waving to lorry as it goes.*) Bye! Bye! Well, (*She
turns to the others.*) that's solved my problem. How
about you?
(*MICHELLE is still waving.*)

BUZZ: Are we here?

BRIAN: Can't be nowhere else. Wherever I am must be
here. But are we here. What did the driver say?

DOLORES: He didn't have time to speak until we stopped. Oh yeah, then he did say this was the place.

BRIAN: Can't be. Can't be.

BUZZ: Where's the hops, Brian? I want to pick hops.

LARRY: Bloody empty fields. Empty bloody fields.

BUZZ: Where's the hops?

MICHELLE: Here hops. Hopscotch. Hopscotch. (*Plays hopscotch.*)

LARRY: Stripped bare. Empty. Nothing. Bloody empty fields, stripped bare. What now?

BRIAN: It can't be the place. There's some mistake.

LARRY: You're the mistake.

DOLORES: Shut up, pukeface!

BRIAN: What month is it?

DOLORES: End of Feb. Month everyone dies.

LARRY: (*Sniffing.*) Smells more like March. Where are these bloody hops you promised?

BRIAN: (*Laughs.*) Sorry, my fault. Wrong season.

DOLORES: Say that again?

BRIAN: Hops ripen September and are picked then. Sorry.

DOLORES: You mean there's no hops?

BRIAN: Sorry, got carried away.

LARRY: But not in a box, unfortunately. Nights under the stars, eh? Thousands of happy singing people drinking glorious ale, eh? I'll give you one o. I'd like to give you one o.

BRIAN: Sorry, really sorry, Dolores. Sorry, Buzz, really sorry. Should have known. My fault. Bloody drugs have burnt my brain away.

LARRY: Why did we follow you? Why was I so bloody stupid?

DOLORES: Christ almighty! Look at us! What a lot of bloody fools we are. We don't deserve to be allowed out.

BRIAN: You're probably right. What came over me? Should have known. Hop-pickers probably don't exist any more. People are redundant. It's all done by machines. I'm so sorry.

DOLORES: What are we going to do?

BRIAN: Only one thing to do. Never go back. Always go forward.

LARRY: Like hell! I've had enough. I'm going back now. Here, Dolores, do you think if we went back Mrs Killick'll be lenient if we said 'We're sorry, Mrs Killick.' 'Ere, what do you think?

DOLORES: Yeah. Larry's right.

LARRY: Come on. What are we waiting for?

MICHELLE: Cold, Dolores, cold…

DOLORES: Yes, darling. Sure you won't come back with us, Brian?

BRIAN: No.

DOLORES: Please come back with us, Brian.

MICHELLE: Please.

LARRY: Come on, Dolores. Let the twit get on with it.

BRIAN: As for me, I'm wending my way to my sister in Southampton. Coming, Buzz?

LARRY: He's an idiot. Let him go.

BRIAN: Come on, Buzz.

BUZZ: Sorry, Brian, you're an idiot.

BRIAN: That's alright. You're right. I wish you all the best of luck in life. Bye for now. (*Waves.*)

LARRY: Come on, Dolores, we've got to get back. We were bloody mad to follow him in the first place.

DOLORES: We were bloody mad in the first place anyway.

BRIAN: I have decided to relinquish my position as cabbage in Margate.

DOLORES: How you going to manage without your happy tabs?

BRIAN: I'll be alright. (*Walking away. Waving. Happy.*) Keep your chin up, everybody. Life could be worth living.

BUZZ: Goodbye, idiot!

DOLORES: You're right. He is a bloody idiot. Good riddance.

BUZZ: Idiot.

LARRY: Spastic.

(*They all go. MICHELLE turns back.*)

MICHELLE: I'll come, Brian.

(*He thinks a moment then ignores her.*)

BRIAN: Toodle-oo. Cheerio. I'll show them. I'm not like other human beings. You can say that again. I AM NOT LIKE OTHER HUMAN BEINGS. I am Brian Singleton and I'm not afraid of anyone. I am not going to be laughed at or stared at any more. Onward!

(*He marches on the spot to inspire himself but can't move anywhere. He sings 'To be a Pilgrim'. Then:*)

Life is beautiful if only you can get into it. I still believe in the human race, God help me. (*Suddenly gripped with pain.*) God help me. (*His pain doubles him. He begins to stumble and fall, then turns the fall into a tango.*) 'Twas all over my jealousy. My crime was just my jealousy.'

(*Suddenly conversationally.*) Dark and light. Dark and light. Dark separates light from light, day from night. Night gives us hope, tomorrow we start again. Where there's death there's hope, yet I love life. I must be mad. I love the earth, I love all creatures on the earth and that includes the human race, which includes myself. I love trees. I love... Mother... I tried to help. I brought you breakfast in bed every morning. Forgive me... BITCH. (*Clasps his hand over his mouth like a ventriloquist's dummy, frightened what may come out if he releases it.*) Why did you bring me into this world? (*Claps his hand over mouth again, then sings.*) 'OH, THE GRAND OLD DUKE OF YORK, HE HAD TEN THOUSAND MEN – HE MARCHED THEM UP TO THE TOP OF THE HILL AND HE MARCHED THEM DOWN AGAIN.' (*Throws himself to the floor doing press-ups, singing as he does so.*) 'No goblin or foul fiend shall daunt his spirit, He knows he at life's end shall inherit. Though fancies flee away... He'll fear not what men say – He'll labour night and day.' No, no. Night and day. No, no. Night and day. Night and day, you are the one, only you beneath the moon and under the stone. 'He'll labour night and day to be a... (*Collapses, exhausted.*) to be a pillbox.' Water, please. I must have water. Thank you, madam, thank you. (*Takes the imaginary water and looks as if he will drink it but pours it over his hands and washes with it.*) I am eternally grateful. Going to pieces, disintegrating, band around my head. (*Suspiciously looks around and slinks over to a phone box. Secretly picks up receiver.*) What?… What?… Oh! Oh there you are. Oh, Jeanette, there you are. I knew you wouldn't let me down. I knew it. There you are. There you are, there you go… What? (*Laughs.*) No… What, when?… No. Did you?… Did you?… Oh? (*Suddenly holds the receiver away, looking at it strangely.*) Well, go to Woolworths then. Go to Woolworths. (*Drops the phone.*) Go to the centre then, go to the centre. Is it dark out? Arthur, Arthur. (*He has rushed madly upstage and flattened himself against the back wall like a wild animal.*) BASTARD! BASTARD! You're right, yes you're right. It's the only answer. Back to Clayton. Yes, get back inside. I promise I won't, I won't, I won't cut my throat. Incidentally haven't you noticed a sudden deterioration in almost everything. Your loving brother, Brian. P.S. washing my hands of this world. Mother, let me in. (*Hammering now on the wall.*) Let me in. Please let me in. (*Stamps his foot.*) Mother, let me in, please let me in.

(*Quietly a strange group has come dancing on. MICHELLE, LARRY, BUZZ, DOLORES, dressed for a wedding. They circle and circle to the wedding march. BRIAN sees them and approaches.*)

Let me in! Please let me in!

(*They dance.*)

LARRY: How's your sister?

BRIAN: Beautiful. Larry! I'm back, don't you see? Let me in!

DOLORES: Let's get on with it.

BRIAN: Hello Buzz. I'm back.

LARRY: Take no notice.

BRIAN: Are you having a party? Can I join in?

DOLORES: You've caused us enough trouble. Leave us alone.

BRIAN: Tell me what's happening. Why are you celebrating?

DOLORES: If you must know, Buzz and me are getting married.

LARRY: But you ain't been invited.

BUZZ: We're getting married. Straight up.

DOLORES: Yeah, straight up over there against the wall.

BRIAN: Please. I'm your friend. You'll let me back in, won't you?

DOLORES: Get lost.

(*They move away. LARRY taunts BRIAN with the cassette.*)

BRIAN: That's mine!

(*BUZZ walks away.*)

DOLORES: Hey, Buzz, where are you going? Come back.

BUZZ: No.

DOLORES: Why not?

BUZZ: Dunno.

DOLORES: But we're getting married.

BUZZ: Changed my mind; you were kidding me, having me on.

DOLORES: Oh, bugger off. (*Seeing BRIAN.*) Hey, why not you?

BRIAN: Please, Dolores, help me get back, give me another chance, I beg you.

DOLORES: Alright, but you'll have to marry me.

BRIAN: Marry you?

DOLORES: Yes, I'm all keyed up, aren't you? I'm all hot and raring to go.

BRIAN: Will Mrs Killick let me in?

DOLORES: I don't know about Mrs Killick, but I certainly will. Come on, I'm all worked up. I can't be thwarted.

BRIAN: Yes, I'm ready. I'm all yours. Thank you, Dolores. I'd marry you any day of the week because deep down you're so nice. Even if I am your second choice. Come on, Larry, get on with it.

LARRY: No, I'm not marrying him. I refuse to officiate.

DOLORES: Well, good riddance then.

LARRY: And good riddance to you too.

DOLORES: You'll have to do it yourself, Brian, because Larry is jealous. Michelle, you can be the witness. Come on, don't look so worried. You might enjoy it. Maybe depravity will be the answer.

BRIAN: No, I'm not sure.

DOLORES: For once in your life, Brian, join in, 'cause if you don't, you're finished. And if you don't mind me saying so, you stink. You need a wash.

BRIAN: I know. It's a bit of an improvement for me, isn't it, forgetting to wash. I'll marry you, Dolores.

LARRY: Alright, I will officiate.

DOLORES: No, it's too late now.

BRIAN: I'll do it myself.

DOLORES: Sod off.

BRIAN: No, let him stay.

LARRY: Well, I'll be you then.

DOLORES: Alright, how can we begin?

BRIAN: Dearly beloved neurotics, oldrotics, maniacs...

DOLORES: Nymphomaniacs...

BRIAN: Quiet! Psychopaths, psychotics... In fact everyone! You and me. You, you and you. The pre-mad, the mad, the post-mad. And those of you who have not yet been diagnosed, those in the throes, and those who pick their nose. Because we all pick our nose, I suppose. We are gathered here under God and the National Health Service...

DOLORES: Oh soon, fantastic fornication in the foam, eh Brian?

BRIAN: Quiet! This is a solemn occasion. By the powers vested in me by my dead mother, William Blake, John Bunyan, God and the devil, I now pronounce us man and strife.

DOLORES: Great!

LARRY: You may now kiss the bride.

DOLORES: Right! Over there. Come on, Brian. Here, this is it.

BRIAN: Oh, my God!

DOLORES: Brian, it's time for goodies. You can't escape one moment longer. Conjugal time is here!

BRIAN: Oh, Mother, this is it!

(*DOLORES pulls him down. The PRIEST sees and rushes over.*)

PRIEST: Stop! Desist! This is an outrage. What are you doing to this man?

BRIAN: It's alright. I'm still a virgin.

PRIEST: Stop it. You should all be ashamed of yourselves!

DOLORES: It was only a bit of a lark.

BRIAN: Sorry.

PRIEST: (*To DOLORES.*) I'm disgusted. Get up! How could you? No wonder this town's sick to death of you lot. I try to defend you and this is how you repay me.

LARRY: Wasn't me.

PRIEST: I am utterly at a loss to know how to deal with you. I try to treat you as normal human beings, but it seems to be useless.

BRIAN: I want to humbly apologise and have a private word with you.

PRIEST: Not now. Not now. Where's Buzz? (*He looks around.*) I'm giving you one last chance. I won't report you to Mrs Killick this time, but I am deeply concerned. I won't have this sort of thing occur ever again. Understood?

(*They all nod.*)

BRIAN: Please can I speak to you? It's urgent.

PRIEST: No, not now.

BRIAN: (*Shouts angrily.*) I must… I must talk to you. You've got to help me.

PRIEST: Alright, Brian. What do you want to say?

BRIAN: I just want to plead for your help. I beg you to ask Mrs Killick to give me another chance. I know I've been a lot of trouble to everyone, but it won't happen again.

PRIEST: (*More kindly.*) Brian, I'm afraid you'll have to come face to face with reality. Listen to me, because someone has to tell you. Whilst you were away we made intensive enquiries about you. Naturally we were concerned. I'm sorry, but you must come down to earth and face up to this. Your sister doesn't exist. For your own reasons you invented her.

BRIAN: (*Quietly.*) I don't believe you.

PRIEST: You must listen to me.

BRIAN: (*Hands over ears.*) Don't want to hear. Don't tell me.

PRIEST: Brian… (*Trying to pull his hands away.*) Brian! If you want my help you must listen to the truth.

BRIAN: Liar! Go away before I kill you.

PRIEST: Do you know? By your refusal to listen you are condemning yourself to everlasting hell; a hell of your own making.

BRIAN: Can't be worse than Margate. She isn't dead. She's in Southampton. She is Jeanette. She is… She does exist. If she doesn't exist, there's no point in living .

PRIEST: God help you, for God knows I can't. (*He goes.*)

BRIAN: I'll never find her now. Never, never.

BUZZ: I'll kill him for you. For doing that to you.

DOLORES: Take no notice. He's a liar.

BRIAN: No, he's not.

BUZZ: I hate him.

BRIAN: Thanks, Buzz.

BUZZ: I hate him for saying that. I hate him. I'm going to get him for that. (*Rushes off.*)

BRIAN: Buzz… (*To DOLORES.*) Will she take me back?

DOLORES: Try.

BRIAN: (*Sits down quietly.*) Dear Jeanette, Goodbye. (*He mimics voices again.*) Happy tabs. What's for dinner? What's on telly? Is it dark out? Is it tomorrow? Go to Woolworths. Got to go to Woolworths. Bastard. Bastard.

LARRY: Flames!

DOLORES: Something's on fire.

LARRY: There's a fire!

MICHELLE: Fire! Fire!

DOLORES: Where's Buzz?

LARRY: It's Dreamland. Dreamland's on fire.

DOLORES: No. It's to the right. Behind Dreamland.

BRIAN: (*Matter of fact.*) It's the church.

MICHELLE: Bonfire! Bonfire!

DOLORES: Oh, my Gawd. It's the church. You're right, it's the bloody church!

(*BUZZ enters looking pleased.*)

BUZZ: It was bigger than the fire at Basingstoke. He made you unhappy. I didn't like that.

BRIAN: Listen, Buzz, whatever you do, don't say a word.

107

LARRY: (*Quietly sings.*) 'Keep the home-fires burning, while
our hearts are yearning...'
(*The PRIEST comes. He is speechless, unable to move.*)
PRIEST: My church, my church, my God!
BRIAN: (*Quietly.*) If he's your God, you're welcome to him.
(*They all just stand there watching the flames.
Later in the hotel. All the residents are lined up before JOAN.
She stops at BRIAN.*)
JOAN: You? You dare to turn up? You dare! And now this.
It's a coincidence, isn't it? Don't you smirk at me.
BRIAN: I wasn't.
JOAN: I'll shove it down your throat. Right, I want the
truth, the whole truth or so help me, I'll skin you alive.
(*The PRIEST is there, sitting stunned. JOHN is also there.
All is quiet.*)
So help me, Reverend, I'm going to get the truth for you.
Now listen to me carefully while there's still time. The
Reverend believes that this terrible tragedy was no
accident. Do you hear me? And I agree with him.
Because I know how you monsters repay the milk of
human kindness.
LARRY: Wasn't us. Swear it on my life. We weren't there.
JOAN: Shut up! Or I'll break every bone in your body.
(*Hits a rolling pin against the table.*) The truth now!
DOLORES: We were getting married. Honest. Brian and
me. Ask the priest. It was all a giggle. We had nothing to
do with it.
JOAN: Quiet! This was a deliberate act. Now, before the
police arrive, I want to know who was responsible. They'll
be here soon, but before they come I am determined to
find the creature. This is your last chance. Do you hear
me? Anyone shielding the criminal will be treated like
a mad criminal and be locked away from humanity.
Because do you know what you have done? You have
practically destroyed the whole rehabilitation process.
I can't believe it. My mind won't really take it in. I am
going to weedle the truth. I am going to get at the truth if
I have to thrash every single one of you.
(*She tugs LARRY's ear. He cringes away.*)
Who is the arsonist? Who? Who?

DOLORES: It was an accident.

PRIEST: It was deliberate. Deliberate. It was an act of arson.

BUZZ: (*Smiling happily.*) I did it, Mrs Killick.

LARRY: No, it wasn't him.

JOAN: (*Shouting at BUZZ.*) It's prison. It's prison for you! Do you hear me?

BRIAN: (*To himself.*) Prison...

BUZZ: I did it 'cause, you know, I like fire. Sorry...

DOLORES: Take no notice. He doesn't know what he's saying.

BUZZ: It was me. Honest. Mike's right. It was deliberate. I did it deliberately. Here are the matches. See? Proof. Sorry, I was cold.

PRIEST: You little rat!

BRIAN: It wasn't Buzz. It was me.

BUZZ: It was me. It was me.

MICHELLE: Me. Me.

BRIAN: It was me.

BUZZ: Brian, it wasn't you.

BRIAN: Yes, it was. Thank you, Buzz.

LARRY: It was Brian. I saw him. It wasn't Buzz. He'd confess to anything. Listen. (*To BUZZ.*) Are you Guy Fawkes?

(*BUZZ nods.*)

Did you burn down the city of London in 1666?

(*BUZZ nods.*)

You see, it was Brian.

BRIAN: Yes. I did it. I did it. I burnt down the church. I burnt the church. I burnt the church. I burnt the church. I burnt the church down, the church down, the church down, I burnt the church down.

LARRY: You should be burnt.

DOLORES: Brian, why have you done this to yourself?

BRIAN: (*To JOAN.*) Did you say I'll go to prison?

JOAN: You'll go to prison, don't you fret.

PRIEST: So this is the way you return Christian charity? You're beyond redemption, do you know that?

BRIAN: Yes, Father. Thank you, Father. Sorry, Dolores. Hope I haven't spoiled anything for you.
(*DOLORES smiles.*)
I hate it out here. Want to go home.

JUDGE: (*Voice-over.*) Society has bent over backwards to help you and people of your kind. In return you repay with total indifference, indulging in scrounging and committing criminal acts of a heinous nature. For this you shall be sent down for five years.

BRIAN: Thank you, sire.

LARRY: You'll be alright in prison. You'll be retrained.

BRIAN: Bye, Buzz. Goodbye, one and all. And the best of luck in life. (*He sings 'Chattanooga Choochoo'.*)

MICHELLE: (*From darkness.*) Bye, bye, Brian.
(*BRIAN continues to sing as he stands in the last fading light. The singing gets more obsessive, more desperate, as light fades.*)

The End.

CALL IN THE NIGHT

Characters

HUGO BAUER

YOUNG HUGO

HATE BRIGADE

MR LEVY

MRS LEVY

MRS BAUER

MR BAUER

KLARA

RUDI

ADELE

YOUNG ADELE

YOUNG WOMAN

SIMON

LOTTE

MR WEBER

MRS WEBER

PETER

WAITER

WAITRESS

GIRL

Call in the Night was first performed at the West Yorkshire Playhouse on 2 May 1995, with the following cast:

HUGO, Gary Waldhorn

YOUNG HUGO, Samuel Mumford

ADELE, Eve Pearce

YOUNG ADELE, Sarah C. Cameron

MR LEVY/MR WEBER, Jeremy Peters

MRS LEVY/MRS WEBER/
MRS BAUER, Jill Brassington

PETER/MR BAUER, John Branwell

SIMON/RUDI/WAITER, Andrew Nyman

KLARA/LOTTE/
YOUNG WOMAN, Tracy-Ann Oberman

Director, Jude Kelly

ACT ONE

Night. A hotel bedroom in Leeds. HUGO enters. He carries a small suitcase and a violin in its case and immediately starts to unpack, placing his clothes in the wardrobe. He takes out a dress-suit, holds it up, considers it, but he does not put this in the wardrobe. Instead he hangs it on the door and stands back, considering it again. Then he washes his hands. He does this with a strange speed and precision.

HUGO: (*Sings softly, cheerfully to himself. Goes to the window, looks out.*) Leeds! God! (*Sings again as he places his small clock and some books on a small bedside table. Then he adjusts the light over his bed. He still quietly hums 'In the Mood' but sometimes the words break through.*) 'In the mood yeah, yeah de-dum-de dum-dum… In the mood oh yeah' (*Goes to the phone.*) Reception? Could you possibly send me up some whisky? If that's not too much trouble… Yes, please. A bottle of Black Label? Johnny Walker. Thank you… How kind… Thank you. (*Puts down the phone, continues to hum to himself, settles himself on the bed and takes up a book. He is about to start reading when the phone rings. He goes and answers it.*) No whisky? Oh?… Really?… This time of night?… I see. Put him through. Mr Scholz! How pleasant… You work late? How on earth did you trace me here?… I see. No. You have not disturbed me. I do apologise. I should have been in touch. But as you know we musicians are always on the move. I should have let you know weeks ago. I hadn't realised the deadline was that close… Yes. I got all your messages. You've been pursuing me for weeks… No, I understand, it's your job. I must apologise… I know I've given you the run-around. Would you please inform Count von Beck that I will respond very soon? And do stress that I am deeply moved that I have been considered for this honour. But he knows that I have not returned to Germany since… since…
(*A knock on the door.*)
Come in!

(*A WAITRESS enters with the whisky. He signals her to place the bottle beside him. The WAITRESS smiles and is about to go.*)

Stay! (*Then he continues his conversation.*) Yes. He understands that this is a big decision for me. Thank you. You're most kind. I shall certainly be in touch, probably no later than tomorrow evening. Is that alright? And I hope I'll be able to accept his generous offer. Thank you. I am deeply, deeply moved. Would you please convey my sincerest and abject apologises to his excellency, also of course my felicitations? Thank you. Goodnight. (*He puts down the phone, blows a raspberry, puts two fingers up and then laughs. Then he turns to the WAITRESS.*)

Well, well. Such service in a provincial hotel. I would be most grateful if you would open it for me.

WAITRESS: Certainly sir.

(*She opens the bottle. He stares at her with some intensity.*)

HUGO: Funny.

WAITRESS: What?

HUGO: I seem to know your face. Maybe we met in another life.

WAITRESS: Yes, sir.

HUGO: I am most obliged. This is for you. (*He gives her a five-pound note.*)

WAITRESS: (*Surprised.*) Thank you, sir.

HUGO: Buy yourself something pretty.

WAITRESS: (*About to go.*) Yes, sir.

HUGO: Are you Irish by any chance?

WAITRESS: Irish?

HUGO: You have a very naughty Irish smile.

WAITRESS: Will that be all, sir?

(*She smiles. We get his meaning. He pours some whisky and drinks it.*)

Goodnight, sir. Thank you.

HUGO: Goodnight. Sleep tight. (*He laughs, pours another glass.*) Down the hatch! (*He drinks. Then he takes up the violin.*)

(*Note: HUGO will hold the instrument as if he were playing, but he will never actually play his violin. Whenever he performs, his hands and arms will not move but will be poised in this static position so that he believes and appears to be playing. In fact the music will always come from another source: his younger self, the YOUNG HUGO, the child he was, the one he can never quite shake off. At other times, when HUGO is blocked and wants to play but cannot, YOUNG HUGO can be otherwise engaged, or be merely having fun, sitting on his hands, or reading a comic, refusing to play for his older self.*)

(*Now he closes his eyes, and plays from the Sibelius violin concerto. It is perfection. Until he remembers something.*) Adele! (*He briskly consults a notebook then takes up the telephone.*) Reception? I would like to make a local call. Yes, please. Leeds 23515. Thank you. (*It rings. Someone answers.*) Adele? Adele! (*He sits down.*) How wonderful to hear your voice. You are an oasis in a desert. Adele! Are you alright?… You sure?… Nonsense. It hasn't been six months. We were in touch, remember? We met in June. I remember distinctly… Kew Gardens. The lilac was out… Surely you know why… It's been advertised. I'm doing a concert here… Tomorrow evening… Adele, I feel so desperately lonely. I thought we could meet. Is that possible?… Just for half an hour. I'm longing to see you. Guess what? You're the first person to know this. I've been invited to Germany. They've offered me a decoration. They want to make me a Knight Commander of the Cross of the Order of Merit of the Federal Republic of Germany… For my services to music, the arts. Humanity. What a gas. Isn't that the most incredible turn up for the books?… I don't know. I've been avoiding going there, that confrontation, all my life. And now it's all exploded in my face… Adele! There is something wrong. Adele! What's going on? (*Silence for a moment.*)

Adele! Please answer. Are you alright? Please. (*She is crying. He covers the phone.*) Shit! (*Into phone.*) Adele! Adele! Please tell me. Tell me… Oh no. Oh no. Poor Henry. My darling Adele, what can I say? Life's not fair… What did they actually say?… I see. Are they sure?… How are you going to cope?… Adele? Adele, be strong. How can I help?... No. My other news doesn't matter. Adele! I need you... No. It isn't all of a sudden. I need you always... To be there... The way you've needed me... I'm at the Grand, of course. I'll call you again. I must see you... Surely I can help you in some way... I can only imagine what you are going through... Goodnight. My thoughts are with you. (*Puts the phone down. Pours another drink.*) Damn him for dying. What am I going to do now? In Leeds? With all this time on my hands? Your own fault, Hugo. Never conjure up the past. (*Drinks and looks out of the window.*) Leeds. It dredges up so much. (*Takes up the violin again and starts playing from the 'Partita' by Bach. But then he hears something. He stops playing but the sound of the violin continues. The other violin plays perfectly. He plays again for a few moments but then he stops, smiles and lies on the bed, drinks more whisky. More at ease, he jokes.*)

I vos born in Dusseldorf and zat is vy they call me Rolf. (*Sings.*) 'Springtime for Hitler and Germany. Deutschland is happy and gay...' *Deutschland über alles.* Down the hatch!

(*But then he decides to put the dress-suit into the wardrobe. He is about to open the wardrobe door when the violin starts playing again, this time from Szymanovski's violin concerto. Opens the wardrobe door wide. A young boy is sitting within, happily playing. This is the YOUNG HUGO, his younger self. The man is not surprised to see the child there.*)

You.

YOUNG HUGO: (*Continues playing.*) You remind me of a man.

HUGO: What man?

YOUNG HUGO: The man with the power.

HUGO: What power?

YOUNG HUGO: The power of the hoodoo.

HUGO: Who do? (*He has enjoyed this game but now he changes his mind.*) The past is dead.

YOUNG HUGO: Is it?

(*HUGO closes the wardrobe door. Inside the playing continues.*)

HUGO: You certainly knew how to play. Then.

(*YOUNG HUGO emerges.*)

What are you doing haunting provincial hotels?

YOUNG HUGO: You opened the door. So, how's life, Hugo?

HUGO: Perfect. Life is a bowl of chicken soup.

YOUNG HUGO: It's tough?

HUGO: What's tough?

YOUNG HUGO: Life.

HUGO: What's life?

YOUNG HUGO: Life's a magazine.

HUGO: How much?

YOUNG HUGO: Ten cents.

HUGO: I haven't got ten cents.

YOUNG HUGO: It's tough.

HUGO: What's tough?

YOUNG HUGO: Life.

(*They both laugh.*)

Life is just here and now. Plus memories. We're meat for the worms.

HUGO: Stop it. Be a child for a change. Instead of the usual smart-arse.

YOUNG HUGO: So what's the problem?

HUGO: Problem? It's overwork. Work. Wear and tear. It's nothing.

YOUNG HUGO: So why the crisis?

HUGO: Crisis?

YOUNG HUGO: Why am I here?

HUGO: You're not. Get lost.

YOUNG HUGO: Suit yourself. (*About to go.*) Hugo, be honest for once in your life.

HUGO: Listen! Everything's perfect. I can assure you. I am at the top of my form.

YOUNG HUGO: So why are you afraid of your mistress?

HUGO: Mistress?

(*YOUNG HUGO lifts up the violin.*)

You're talking out of your toches.

YOUNG HUGO: Hugo, what do you fear?

HUGO: Only myself.

YOUNG HUGO: Exactly. Hugo, be honest. You're afraid that your fingers won't obey you.

HUGO: Fuck off. Stupid little sod.

YOUNG HUGO: Come on. You can't fool me. I was there.

HUGO: Where?

YOUNG HUGO: Queen Elizabeth Hall. The South Bank. Three weeks ago. You only just managed to control it.

HUGO: I was tired. I need rest. Listen!

(*He nods at YOUNG HUGO, takes up his violin. YOUNG HUGO smiles and takes up his violin. HUGO, poised in playing mode, goes into Paganini's 'Caprice' with immaculate ease. All his radiant confidence is there.*)

So? Clever little shit. What's wrong with that?

YOUNG HUGO: Beautiful. Brilliant. You haven't lost our touch. Not entirely.

HUGO: Thank you. So why haunt me?

YOUNG HUGO: Who's haunting who? You opened the door. (*He is about to re-enter the wardrobe. But then he hesitates.*) Hugo, you've forgotten how to smile. Please!

HUGO: You always were an appealing little bastard. Alright.

YOUNG HUGO: Great. I'm good at this. I'll throw you one. (*He fixes a big smile to his face then wipes it off with his hand and throws it across the room to his older self.*) Don't drop it. No! Here's another. Catch!

(*HUGO immediately catches the smile, fixes it to his face and then throws it back to his younger self. They continue like this, in slow motion, throwing the smile like a frisbee, one to the other. They laugh. Meanwhile the wardrobe has increased in size and now occupies a more prominent position in the room. Others now emerge from the wardrobe. HUGO sees them and stops playing. Note: these figures will appear throughout the play in various guises.*)

HUGO: I don't want them.

YOUNG HUGO: Fair enough.

(*The figures return into the wardrobe. YOUNG HUGO is about to follow them.*)

HUGO: Wait! I want you around. It's lonely in Leeds.

YOUNG HUGO: Take me, take the lot. You can't pick and choose.

HUGO: I absolutely refuse to have them as well.

YOUNG HUGO: We'll see.

HUGO: Yes, we will. (*He snaps his fingers. The shadows melt away.*) There! Who's in command?

YOUNG HUGO: (*Bows.*) Your Majesty.

HUGO: Basically I don't need anyone.

YOUNG HUGO: Absolutely.

HUGO: It's just my mind. I've been drinking a little too much of late. (*He drinks. Takes up the violin.*) I'm lonely. Life is lonely. We're all on our own. (*He places his ear to the violin.*) I need something. Someone. Listen. (*He puts the violin to YOUNG HUGO's ear.*) Can't you hear?

YOUNG HUGO: No. Just your voice, reverberating.

HUGO: They're all locked in here? Their songs. Their language. Their laughter, their cries. Listen! Harmonics of death.

YOUNG HUGO: I hear nothing, Hugo. The wind maybe.

HUGO: The wind. Isn't that enough?

YOUNG HUGO: I'm afraid you're a wailing wall Yid, Hugo.

HUGO: I'm a survivor.

YOUNG HUGO: Then get on with living, my old son. Make music.

HUGO: The violin. It is my life. My death. My breath. My heartbeat. I'm so afraid. I hate this instrument. It is not behaving.

YOUNG HUGO: Hugo. What's the problem? You take up your violin, thus, and you play. (*A few bars of 'Lark Ascending' by Vaughan Williams.*) Easy.

HUGO: 'Lark Ascending.' But smoke gets in my eyes.

YOUNG HUGO: I'm starving.

HUGO: The better you play, the closer you get to the abyss. Must phone my wife. Our wife.

(*YOUNG HUGO is about to return to the wardrobe. HUGO snaps his fingers.*)

Don't go.

YOUNG HUGO: I am yours.

HUGO: Maybe I dreamed it. Maybe she hasn't left me. (*He dials.*) Sylvie? You're there… (*Relieved.*) I told you. Leeds… Sylvie! Listen. It's absurd. Thirty-four years together. A lifetime… You can't. Not now… Sylvie! You're a grandmother… It doesn't make sense… He's twenty years younger than you... Alright. Look! Have your fling... (*She clicks off.*) Sylvie? (*He slams the receiver down.*) Bitch. Why does she want to destroy me? (*He turns to YOUNG HUGO.*) Why?

(*YOUNG HUGO shrugs.*)

YOUNG HUGO: (*Suddenly unhappy.*) I want to go home.

HUGO: Where's home?

YOUNG HUGO: I want to go home.

HUGO: Cheer up. You're a long time dead. (*He gets down on the floor and cuddles YOUNG HUGO.*) Come on. Good boy.

YOUNG HUGO: I'm nowhere. I'm lost.

HUGO: Ha ha ha! You were such a cocky little sod a few minutes ago.

YOUNG HUGO: I want to go home. Take me home.

HUGO: Listen! Guess where we are? I bet you don't know where we are.

YOUNG HUGO: I do.

HUGO: Where? Where are we?

YOUNG HUGO: In a room.

HUGO: But where?

YOUNG HUGO: In the world.

HUGO: Hugo, we're in Leeds. Out there is Leeds.

YOUNG HUGO: Leeds?

HUGO: Where we once lived. Down there. Those streets. The map to the past. Come with me, come on. Let's retrace our steps? Good idea? Cling to me. That's right. I'm all you've got. You're all I've got. Remember the Levys?

YOUNG HUGO: No.

HUGO: You will. They could remind us of many things. Some clues leading to all this... dark passage of time. Our lives are bound up in this place... In those streets. Hey! Could they still be alive? Impossible. Pass me that telephone book.

(*YOUNG HUGO gives him the directory.*)

Surely they must be under the earth now. Grinning away, for all eternity.

YOUNG HUGO: You're so morbid. I don't want to be here.

HUGO: Neither do I.

YOUNG HUGO: I'll have nightmares.

HUGO: Bound to be dead. By now. Still. Worth a try. Yes? Try. Number. Number. Number. (*Flips through the telephone directory.*) Levy! Levy! Levy! Doctor Maurice Levy! Still listed. The same. Yes! Twenty-seven Roundhay Park Road. God. Still alive. In the midst of death we are in life. *Selah*! (*Dials.*) Cold?

YOUNG HUGO: Cold? No.

HUGO: Then stop shivering.

(*Someone answers at the other end.*)

Hello! Is that Doctor Levy's household?... May I speak with the doctor?... Or his wife... Oh! I'm a friend. From the past. You?... Who are you?... Grandson! But they never had children, did they?... Oh! I see. Tell me, are they still alive?... Really? Marvellous. May I speak... Where?... Oh! Are they alright?... Really? That's wonderful news. What's their address?... Please! May I write this down... I would love to visit them... (*He writes.*) Thank you. You have been most kind. (*He puts the phone down.*) We're going.

YOUNG HUGO: You remind me of a man.

HUGO: What man?

YOUNG HUGO: The man with the power.

HUGO: What power?

YOUNG HUGO: The power of the hoodoo.

HUGO: Who do?

YOUNG HUGO: You do.

HUGO: I do what?

YOUNG HUGO: You remind me of a man.

YOUNG HUGO: I'm starving.

HUGO: You don't exist.

YOUNG HUGO: I don't exist because I'm hungry.

HUGO: Come. Kosher food.

YOUNG HUGO: Where?

HUGO: Springfield. Retirement home for Jewish skeletons. (*Sings.*) 'Gotta take a sentimental journey...' You got me into this, Hugo. 'To renew old memories...'

(*They enter the wardrobe. The night streets of Leeds pour out of the wardrobe. The figures appear again but this time they have identity, have become the HATE BRIGADE, a phalanx*

of skinhead youth. HUGO enters, seems scared of the lurking
youths (both sexes). He looks around for his younger self.
YOUNG HUGO is nowhere.)

He stirs me up, then disappears. (*He calls.*) Hugo!
(*The HATE BRIGADE laugh.*)
The contagion was merely dormant.

HATE BRIGADE: *Sieg heil! Sieg heil!* Keep Britain white!
Out with foreigners! Out with the niggers! Out with the
Yids! Out with the Pakis! *Sieg heil! Sieg heil! Sieg heil!*
Out with the Yids!

HUGO: If I knew of another world.

HATE BRIGADE: (*Encircling him. Chanting.*) Jew boy! Jew
boy! Jew boy!

HUGO: All my life I believed in democracy. But if I had
a gun… Bastards. Bastards. Hugo! You got me into this.
Stop playing fast and loose.

HATE BRIGADE: (*Faces contorted.*) JEW BOY! JEW
BOY! JEW!

HUGO: (*Takes out a little mirror and inspects his face.*) Didn't
think I looked particularly Jewish.
(*Quickly combs his hair, hurries on and enters 'Springfield*
Home' which has appeared before him. There in the lounge
HUGO witnesses the scene arranging itself. Old people enter
and sit silently, staring into space. These are 'the figures' who
will constantly take on various identities. Suddenly the residents
spontaneously break out into feeble community singing.)

ALL: 'Oh we'll all go together. All go together, all go
together when we go. Singing I-yi-yippy-yippy-I-singing-
I-yi-yippy-yippy-I. Singing I-yi-yippy-I-yi-yippy-I-yi-
yippy-yippy-I-'
(*They stop suddenly and as one they resume their catatonic*
state. HUGO approaches a couple who are sitting opposite
each other. They both wear soft smiles fixed to their faces.)

HUGO: Hello. Do you remember me?

MR LEVY: Hello. Do you remember me?

MRS LEVY: Hello. Do you remember me? I loved him.

MR LEVY: Who?

MRS LEVY: I don't remember.

HUGO: I lived with you. I'm Hugo Bauer. Hugo.

MR LEVY: Hugo?

MRS LEVY: Hugo? Must Hu go? Hugo.

HUGO: (*Taking up the violin.*) This might jog your memory.

MR LEVY: He's a fiddler.

MRS LEVY: Wish he'd fiddle with me.

HUGO: What happened? You were both so quiet. Nice. Respectable.

(*They laugh raucously.*)

What life does to us?

MRS LEVY: Play *Rosinkers mit Mandlen.* (*She sings.*) *Rosinkers mit Mandlen.* Dum, dum, dum. *Mit Mandlen.*

(*She and MR LEVY dance slowly, weaving around each other.*) Play!

(*MR LEVY plays the Yiddish song.*)

MR LEVY: Why is he here?

MRS LEVY: Search me?

MR LEVY: In front of everyone? (*Tickles her and she lies on the floor giggling like a child. MR LEVY searches, putting his hand up her clothes.*)

HUGO: (*Interrupting.*) What was I like as a child? What was it like really? Listen! I lived with you. For Christ's sake, listen. What was I like as a child?

(*They sit down, quiet again.*)

MRS LEVY: You were very happy.

MR LEVY: Always smiling, never a moment's trouble.

MRS LEVY: A clever, gifted, sweet angelic child.

MR LEVY: A gifted little boy from Germany.

(*We hear a terrible drum-like reverberation. HUGO pulls back a tablecloth. He is pleased to see YOUNG HUGO sitting there, banging his fists against the floor. But the LEVYS are never aware of the YOUNG HUGO.*)

MRS LEVY: (*To HUGO.*) Hugo. My lovely little chap. Come here, my darling. My genius. (*She goes to HUGO and cuddles him. She smells. He shudders.*) Of course I remember you, darling boy, lovely little Hugo.

YOUNG HUGO: (*Under table.*) I want my mother. I want my mother. I want my mother.

MRS LEVY: (*Still cuddling HUGO in a relentless grip.*) Come to me. Come to me. Come. Never a moment's trouble. My sweet little darling boy.

YOUNG HUGO: (*Under table.*) I want my mother. I want my mother.

HUGO: (*To YOUNG HUGO under the table.*) Big brave boy. Pull yourself together.

YOUNG HUGO: She kept the others with her. She sent me away.

MR LEVY: There! There! My pretty boy.
(*They both hold HUGO tight in a strangle-hold.*)

YOUNG HUGO: I will not be chosen. Don't send me away. I want my mother.

HUGO: Leave me alone. I must get out of here. (*He frantically tries to free himself. He punches MRS LEVY, pulls her hair.*)

MRS LEVY: (*Snarling.*) Get him out of here. Get him out.

MR LEVY: Get the little bastard out of here.

MR LEVY/MRS LEVY: (*Roar.*) Out! Out!

RESIDENTS: (*Roar.*) Out! Out!
(*HUGO pulls the laughing YOUNG HUGO out from under the table.*)

YOUNG HUGO: (*Mocking, poking out his tongue.*) Big, brave boy.

HUGO: I'm ashamed of you. Come!

MRS LEVY: (*Now sweet.*) Bye bye Hugo.

RESIDENTS: (*Smiling and waving.*) Bye bye.

HUGO: (*Mocking YOUNG HUGO, pretending to cry.*) I want my mother. I want my mother. Oh Lord, thou pluckest me, burning, burning.
(*He carries the struggling YOUNG HUGO off into the dark. All the RESIDENTS immediately go back into a singsong.*)

RESIDENTS: 'Oh we'll all go together. All go together, all go together when we go. Singing I-yi-yippy-yippy-I-singing-I-yi-yippy-yippy-I. Singing I-yi-yippy-I-yi-yippy-I-yi-yippy-yippy-I-'
(*As one they resume their catatonic state, standing in a circle, making appropriate gestures. They become tribal, atavistic, grotesque. The scene disappears into the wardrobe and HUGO and YOUNG HUGO emerge into the hotel bedroom.*)

HUGO: I was managing and then you spoilt everything.

YOUNG HUGO: (*Quietly.*) I want my mother. I want my mother.

HUGO: Yes. She was the most beautiful woman. The only woman. I breathe her in. I loved her.

YOUNG HUGO: Liar! You hated her.

HUGO: You remind me of a man.

YOUNG HUGO: Not playing.

HUGO: You remind me of a man.

YOUNG HUGO: What man?

HUGO: The man with the answer?

YOUNG HUGO: What answer?

HUGO: You give me the question, I'll give you the answer.

YOUNG HUGO: I want my mother. I don't want to be chosen. How could she do that to me? I'm starving.

HUGO: Children should be obscene and not absurd. Play!

YOUNG HUGO: You play?

HUGO: I'll put you back in the dark.

YOUNG HUGO: (*Laughs.*) Yes, please.

HUGO: Later.

YOUNG HUGO: You'll be lucky. (*Plays 'Partita Number Three' by Bach.*)

HUGO: I hate music.

YOUNG HUGO: Now he tells me. (*Quietly.*) I want my mother.

(*Continues to play. HUGO opens the door and he is in the empty streets of Leeds. He whistles and YOUNG HUGO follows him, still playing. They creep slowly until a huge Nazi flag unfurls from the top of a building. Drums sound. They are in the empty streets of Berlin. It is 1939. The drumming gets louder and louder until it becomes deafening. They run until they enter the room of the past. HUGO's Berlin home. YOUNG HUGO still has his violin. He plays. Figures emerge and when YOUNG HUGO stops playing they applaud warmly. Then the atmosphere changes. MRS BAUER, HUGO's mother, approaches, followed by KLARA, his sister, and his young brother, RUDI. They stand close together. HUGO's father is not there. MRS BAUER approaches HUGO.*)

MRS BAUER: Kurt! Say something. Kurt! (*HUGO realises he has been cast into being his own father. He has no choice.*)

HUGO: (*As Mr Bauer.*) It is invidious. To have to choose.

MRS BAUER: Kurt! We have already chosen.

HUGO: (*As Mr Bauer.*) To have to choose. This is their worst crime.

MRS BAUER: At least one of us will have a chance.

HUGO: (*As Mr Bauer.*) Darling. Shouldn't we all stay together?

MRS BAUER: Kurt! We have made up our mind.

HUGO: (*As Mr Bauer.*) Have we? Rudi?

MRS BAUER: We've discussed this. Far too young.

HUGO: (*As Mr Bauer.*) Klara?

MRS BAUER: Far too frail. Hugo is the right age. It must be Hugo.

HUGO: (*As Mr Bauer.*) Yes. You're right. It's got to be Hugo.

MRS BAUER: (*Turning to YOUNG HUGO, cuddling him.*) Darling.

YOUNG HUGO: Why? Why are you sending me away?

MRS BAUER: Hugo! You have been chosen.

YOUNG HUGO: Don't you love me any more?

MRS BAUER: Darling. You have a special gift and you must give it to the world.

YOUNG HUGO: I don't want the world. I want you.

HUGO: (*As Mr Bauer.*) Hugo. Be happy. You are going to England.

YOUNG HUGO: No.

HUGO: (*As Mr Bauer.*) It's all been decided.

MRS BAUER: We have no other choice.

YOUNG HUGO: Mother?

(*He goes towards her, wanting to embrace her. She is about to cry, but is being disciplined.*)

MRS BAUER: Hugo! Pull yourself together.

(*He doesn't and starts to sob.*)

YOUNG HUGO: Cow!

(*She slaps him on the face and then hurries off, crying.*)

HUGO: (*As Mr Bauer.*) How dare you talk to your mother like that!

YOUNG HUGO: Mother! Mother! (*He then turns on his father, shaking with fury.*) Coward! (*Then picking up his violin.*) My curse. (*He lifts it above his head, ready to smash it down.*)

HUGO: (*As Mr Bauer.*) Give me that violin.

YOUNG HUGO: I'll give it to you.

(*MRS BAUER returns.*)

MRS BAUER: Hugo!

YOUNG HUGO: I don't want to go away. I want to die with you.

MRS BAUER: No one's going to die.

YOUNG HUGO: Why should you all die without me?

KLARA: (*Softly.*) Hugo.

(*KLARA holds out her hand. YOUNG HUGO gives the violin to her. And cries. MRS BAUER tries to comfort her son but YOUNG HUGO stands back in fury. The crowd of watching figures becomes the HATE BRIGADE.*)

YOUNG HUGO: (*Pointing his finger at his father and his mother.*) You! You!

MRS BAUER: (*Commanding him to stop his fury.*) Boy! Boy!

YOUNG HUGO: You! You!

HUGO: (*As Mr Bauer.*) Boy! Boy!

ALL: You boy! You boy! You boy! (*The HATE BRIGADE mis-hear his words; slowly starts to encircle the man and boy.*)

HATE BRIGADE: (*Quietly at first, but building to a crescendo.*) Jew! Jew! Boy! Boy! Jew boy! Jew boy! Jew boy! Jew boy! (*YOUNG HUGO gets caught up in the hate, joins in, enjoys screaming at his father.*)

YOUNG HUGO: Jew boy! Jew boy! Jew boy! Jew boy! (*HUGO as Mr Bauer stands with his wife and daughter, withering in the centre of the mob. But now the mob melt away. YOUNG HUGO becomes himself again.*)

(*Quietly.*) I am not going. I refuse to be the chosen.

(*KLARA and RUDI run off.*)

MRS BAUER: All understanding has left this world.

(*She goes off. HUGO as Mr Bauer sits, head in hands.*)

HUGO: (*Takes up the violin, becomes himself again.*) Every musician in the world comes face to face with this wall, sooner or later.

(*The phone rings. He quickly answers it. We are back in the Leeds hotel.*)

Adele! Thank God. I was miles away. How is he?...

I see... I see. Can you at least come to the concert?...

Adele! I'm... having problems... Can't explain... Not

over the phone. I need your moral support... I'm afraid... Try... I'd love to see your face in that audience; an oasis in that sea of faces... I see... I understand... Afterwards?... You will?... Better than nothing. Even fifteen minutes... Where? (*Makes a note.*) 'Happy Hour Wine Bar, Briggate.' Very close to the hospital... Good. Adele! I need you now more than ever... The concert should be over by ten. See you there ten thirty... Wait for me. I love you. I'm sorry... Bye. (*Puts the phone down then lifts it again.*) Reception? I ordered a meal... Hours ago. Would it be too much trouble if it arrived? Thank you. You are most kind. (*Takes up the violin.*) They died with her. But because I could play this cursed thing she sent me away. Do I dare and do I dare? Shall we?
(*YOUNG HUGO, sitting on the bed, takes up his violin. HUGO plays perfectly from Bloch's violin concerto. There is a knock on the door.*)
Enter!
(*HUGO continues playing. One of the figures enters. Dressed as a waiter he brings a trolley of food and sets the table.*)

WAITER: May I say that I am honoured to serve such an eminent person.

HUGO: (*Stops playing.*) Thank you. You are most kind. (*The man goes and HUGO starts to eat, but YOUNG HUGO watches him too intently. HUGO suddenly pushes the food away and quickly starts shaving, using a cut-throat razor. The ravenous YOUNG HUGO falls upon the food.*)
If only I were invisible. A lifetime of being pointed at makes me sick. They want to touch you. They think you have been touched by the gods. I have been touched alright. (*Gets into his dress-suit, ready for the concert.*) The dead hate me. (*Brushing his hair.*) I'm ready.
(*YOUNG HUGO takes HUGO's hand and pulls him through the dark to a railway station.*)
You've brought me to the wrong place. Take me back. We're late for the concert.
(*But it is too late. It is Berlin, 1939. His family are there, standing in smoke. MRS BAUER approaches him.*)
I don't want to be here. Take me back. Take me back.

MRS BAUER: Kurt! There you are!

(*HUGO becomes his father once again.*)

HUGO: (*As Mr Bauer. Turning to YOUNG HUGO.*) So, we are being very brave.

YOUNG HUGO: Are we?

KLARA: Isn't it exciting? The new Yasha Heifitz is going to astound London.

YOUNG HUGO: I'm starving.

KLARA: Goodbye, Hugo.

YOUNG HUGO: Goodbye, Klara. Goodbye Father.

HUGO: (*As Mr Bauer.*) Goodbye, Hugo.

(*They shake hands.*)

YOUNG HUGO: Goodbye, Mother.

MRS BAUER: Goodbye, Hu… My son.

(*Cuddles him. He sways against her within the embrace. Then pulls away.*)

YOUNG HUGO: I'll never forgive you for this.

MRS BAUER: I understand. Of course you're emotional. My darling…

KLARA: Hurry. The train…

HUGO: (*As Mr Bauer.*) Never forget who you are.

MRS BAUER: You're Jewish, no matter what the cost. I love you.

YOUNG HUGO: Really?

HUGO: Let's go. Let's get away from here.

(*The family back into the wardrobe and YOUNG HUGO starts to close it.*)

MRS BAUER: Take this with you. (*She produces a small menorah.*) The light of our faith.

YOUNG HUGO: (*Taking the sacred candlestick.*) Faith in what?

MRS BAUER: I don't know. Faith in faith. Go, Hugo. Go for all of us.

YOUNG HUGO: (*He holds up the menorah.*) I don't understand.

MRS BAUER: What don't you understand?

YOUNG HUGO: I don't understand what I don't understand.

MRS BAUER: Who understands? Goodbye.

(*The family disappear in smoke. In the Leeds hotel, YOUNG HUGO is going through the luggage. He takes out the menorah and gives it to HUGO.*)

HUGO: (*Holding the menorah high.*) She gave me this and sent me away. On the one hand my Jewishness. On the other my banishment. Mother! I didn't want the world. I wanted you. I wanted to die with you. Not live without you.
(*YOUNG HUGO eats voraciously.*)
That's all you care about. All my life I've tried to throw it away.

YOUNG HUGO: (*Grabbing the menorah, he throws it out of the window.*) Gone. (*Then he comes to inspect HUGO.*) Have a good concert. Play like the devil. It's hard.

HUGO: What's hard?

YOUNG HUGO: If it ain't hard I'm sorry for you, old man. It's tough.

HUGO: What's tough?

YOUNG HUGO: Existence.

HUGO: What's existence?

YOUNG HUGO: A bowl of cherries.

HUGO: I ain't got a bowl of cherries.

YOUNG HUGO: It's hard. Dadar! (*Now a conjurer, he produces the menorah from HUGO's cloak and stands it on a table. HUGO laughs.*) There! You're ready. Play well.

HUGO: (*Steps forward and stands before us, the concert audience.*) I will now play Alban Berg's Violin Concerto. This is known as 'Night Music.' Our age is night. This was written in memoriam for the death of Manon Werfel, daughter of Alma Mahler. I dedicate this performance to my sister Klara, whose smile is now but dust. (*Begins to play but soon falters. Puts his ear to the violin.*) They live in here. They laugh and cry in here. I was chosen to survive because I was cursed with talent. Fame is a cage. An audience is a thing. A devouring thing. Sorry. Not feeling too well. Not myself tonight. I beg your indulgence. I cannot continue with this concert. (*Quickly leaves and immediately is back in the hotel room. Sits on the bed, dazed.*)

YOUNG HUGO: Smile! Here! I'll throw you one.
(*Throws a smile but HUGO doesn't respond.*)
It's hard.

(*HUGO doesn't respond. YOUNG HUGO talks to himself.*)
What's hard? – Life. What's life? – Life's an obstacle
race. Can you win? – No. In the end you fall on your
arse. No redemption? – No. No resurrection? – No.
Winners. Losers. Christians. Jews. Bookmakers.
Ayatollas. Pimps. All of us. Into the earth. It's hard.
Especially in winter. (*He looks at his watch.*) Time to kill.
Time to kill again. Two hours before I meet her. Hugo!
How do you kill time? – Read the *Yorkshire Post*.

HUGO: (*He opens the papers and reads.*) Aha! Funny. An
ex- minister of Her Majesty's government claims that the
Holocaust may not have happened. So, did you know,
young Hugo, that our family have been on holiday in
Disneyworld for the past fifty-two years, enjoying
themselves too much to even send a postcard. (*Laughs.*)
Now tell me that I'm over-sensitive. Obsessed. Nothing's
been learned.
(*A fire engine is heard.*)
In his mind the survivor sees everyone else erecting
scaffolds in the streets. It couldn't happen here, could
it, not in Leeds? Two hours to kill. In Leeds. How
inconsiderate of her. And her nice husband on the
blink. How could you do this to me?
(*HUGO sits on the bed. In the corner YOUNG HUGO plays
Vaughan Williams' 'Lark Ascending'. Suddenly we are near
a derelict shed near the edge of the sea. In the distance, children
sing 'If you're happy and you know it clap your hands'.*)
The day we arrived in Felixstowe. Remember the
transit camp?
(*YOUNG ADELE approaches. She watches YOUNG HUGO
as he plays. But then, sensing someone is there, he stops and
turns to her.*)

YOUNG ADELE: Hello.

YOUNG HUGO: Hello.

YOUNG ADELE: How do you do?

YOUNG HUGO: I'm not sure, thank you very much.

YOUNG ADELE: My name is Adele.

YOUNG HUGO: My name is Hugo.
(*They shake hands.*)

YOUNG ADELE: You too came from Germany?

YOUNG HUGO: Yes.

YOUNG ADELE: You too were chosen?

YOUNG HUGO: I have finished talking to you.

YOUNG ADELE: Why are you crying?

YOUNG HUGO: I'm not. Go away. (*Plays again.*)

YOUNG ADELE: You are very clever.

YOUNG HUGO: Yes, I am.

YOUNG ADELE: I feel sad and wonderful. What is the tune?

YOUNG HUGO: 'Lark Ascending.' By Ralph Vaughan Williams. An English composer. Now, go. You are disturbing my concentration.

YOUNG ADELE: May I just stand here and listen to you?

YOUNG HUGO: It is of no concern of mine what you do. As long as you do not speak to me ever again. Thank you. (*He continues playing.*)

(*Thunder and lightning strike the night sky. He continues to play and she continues to stand there. Then it is morning. Then dark. Then light again.*)

Good morning.

YOUNG ADELE: Good morning. Did you sleep well?

YOUNG HUGO: I do not sleep.

YOUNG ADELE: The sky is very blue at this particular moment.

(*No reply.*)

So, we are in England?

YOUNG HUGO: Yes.

YOUNG ADELE: And where is our final destination?

YOUNG HUGO: I am not concerned.

YOUNG ADELE: Heaven? That is where our families may go.

YOUNG HUGO: Our families may go to hell. Especially my mother.

YOUNG ADELE: That's wicked.

YOUNG HUGO: Yes. I must be wicked. They sent me away. We are going to Leeds today.

YOUNG ADELE: Leeds?

YOUNG HUGO: It is situated in the suburbs of Hull, I believe.

YOUNG ADELE: Isn't that where the devil lives?

YOUNG HUGO: The devil lives everywhere, these days.

YOUNG ADELE: Hugo, we will never see our families again.

YOUNG HUGO: Now I will play the Gavotte by Johann Sebastian Bach. (*He does.*)

YOUNG ADELE: That is the most beautiful sound I ever heard.

YOUNG HUGO: I am going to be the greatest violinist in the world. What are you going to be?

YOUNG ADELE: Human.

YOUNG HUGO: Some of my best friends are human.

HUGO: Play, Hugo. It covers the pain.

YOUNG HUGO: I prefer the pain.

HUGO: Play!

YOUNG HUGO: I'll throw you one.

(*He does and HUGO adopts a terrible smile-mask.*)

HUGO: Let's go.

YOUNG HUGO: Where?

HUGO: The concert.

YOUNG HUGO: We're there.

HUGO: Where?

YOUNG HUGO: Through here.

(*They walk into the wardrobe and are in the concert hall.*)

HUGO: Moloch! Look at it. Who let it in? The monster. The audience. Save me from it. It believes music redeems. The closest it will ever get to God. Doesn't it know God is tone deaf? He hates music. So do I. The audience spoils everything. The musicians alone, with their instruments… ah well, that is something different. Why am I so afraid that I will be swallowed by the great beast? Look! Moloch! And so it is all over the world. I travel. If it's doomsday I must be in Montreal. Or Tokyo. Rio de Janeiro. Or homeless. In the air, going where? Up in smoke? Where was I? Where am I? Where will I be tomorrow? Where am I tonight? Ladies and gentlemen, it is my great pleasure, my privilege to be here with you in your wonderful shining city of – of – of – (*Panicking.*) Where the hell am I? (*Whispers.*) Where am I?

YOUNG HUGO: Leeds.

HUGO: Ladies and gentlemen. Good citizens of Leeds.
Tonight it is my pleasure to play for you. I shall play…
(*YOUNG HUGO laughs.*)
What? Play, you little bastard. Play!

YOUNG HUGO: Sorry. I left my violin back at the hotel.
(*He leaves.*)

HUGO: (*To the audience.*) Ladies and gentlemen. I beg your
indulgence. I don't know how to put this. I am desperately
sorry. Forgive me. I am under strain. I cannot proceed.
I am not myself tonight. Please? Klara! Rudi! Mother.
Forgive me. I am somewhere else.
(*Looks at his watch and walks into the Happy Hour Wine
Bar where somnambulist dancers slowly grind around the
room to punky soulsounds. YOUNG HUGO and YOUNG
ADELE are already there. Watching, smoking, giggling.*)
You little bastard.
(*ADELE enters. A middle-aged, plump, sexy lady. They
embrace.*)
How long have you got?

ADELE: Half an hour.

HUGO: Come to my hotel.

ADELE: No time.

HUGO: Time enough…

ADELE: When the prick stands, the brain dies.

HUGO: Roll on, brain death. How's Henry? Still dying
with such good humour?

ADELE: I can't face it.

HUGO: If only he were a bastard.

ADELE: I don't want to talk about him. How was
the concert?

HUGO: Fantastic. They loved me.

ADELE: Good. They always do.

HUGO: It was abysmal, Adele. I didn't play. I couldn't.

ADELE: I don't understand.

HUGO: Adele. (*Sings.*) 'My hands are not connecting to my
thighbones. My thighbones not connecting to my head
bone…' My hands are in revolt. I can't get through
to them.

ADELE: Hugo, what's going on? Tell me.

HUGO: Have you got a year? Adele, I have this urge to chuck it. To throw it away.

ADELE: Life? The family?

HUGO: The violin. Anyway, they got their money back, I believe.

ADELE: But music is your life.

HUGO: Exactly. I'm under great stress.

ADELE: Self-indulgence is a luxury I can't afford.

HUGO: Thank you so very much for your understanding.

ADELE: I'm sorry. Forgive me?

HUGO: Of course.

ADELE: It's all happened so suddenly.

HUGO: Nothing does. It's been creeping up on me. The offer from Germany was the last straw. I can't go.

ADELE: Hugo. You must. It's such an honour.

HUGO: They've been after me for weeks. I've been avoiding them. I'm so afraid. Look at my hands. Mutinous bastards. I'll be alright. It happens. I promised to return to Leeds in a few weeks to do the concert when it all blows over. The audience were very nice. They understood. I do owe them something. Dance with me.

ADELE: No. Just sit.

YOUNG HUGO: Adele?

(*YOUNG HUGO and YOUNG ADELE dance with the others but keep another tempo: more like jitterbugging to slow moody blues. The WAITRESS comes with their drinks.*)

WAITRESS: Chaardonnaaaay.

HUGO: Thank you. (*To ADELE.*) Can't you stay a little longer? I'm lost. Would you believe it? The last train to London already gone. Leeds at night. What a prospect! The town centre. The nightlife! You wouldn't believe it. How did you manage to get away?

ADELE: 'You need some fresh air,' she said. 'Go home for an hour. Put your feet up. We'll call you if there's any change.' My daughters, Sharon and Sandra, are there with their husbands.

HUGO: We have got time, you know. You need me.

ADELE: Yes. Just hold me.

(*He stands and she falls into his arms. They embrace. Then he slowly starts to dance, coaxing her. She follows automatically.*)

HUGO: Please. To the hotel.

ADELE: That's all you're good for. Fucking and fiddling.

HUGO: Not sure about the fiddling. (*Referring to his younger dancing self.*) He's visiting me.

ADELE: Who?

HUGO: The boy. My childhood.

ADELE: (*Takes his glass, puts it down.*) Strong stuff.

HUGO: She's also there. With them?

ADELE: Who?

HUGO: You.

ADELE: Nothing surprises me any more.

HUGO: I mean it. We're dancing.

ADELE: Of course we are.

HUGO: We're dancing over there.

ADELE: Nothing to worry about. You're just going mad.

HUGO: If this is a sane world, thank God I'm going mad. (*Does some mad steps.*)

ADELE: You always were. So tell me, why am I still attracted to you?

HUGO: Why am I still so excited by you? You move me. Come on, Adele. You want it.

ADELE: Imagine. A respectable middle-aged grandmother from Leeds being propositioned by a genius.

HUGO: Careful with that word. Adele. I want you. I want to marry you.

ADELE: Yes, yes. I know what you want.

HUGO: I mean it. I want to marry you.

ADELE: Hugo, that time has passed. I'm also mad, dancing here with you… and my… my poor – Henry! I must go…

HUGO: Wait! We must talk. Sensibly.

ADELE: You? Sensible?

HUGO: Adele. We must be practical.

ADELE: You? Practical?

HUGO: We still have some life to live. Henry wants that.

ADELE: I won't hear this.

HUGO: Adele! I'm free. I've done it.

ADELE: Liar!

HUGO: I finally found the courage. It's all over between Sylvie and me. I swear. I need you. I'm desperate.

ADELE: Hugo! You are such a con man. You're wealthy. You travel. People adore you, pamper you, hang on to your words. When you call you expect us all to go running. You are a lucky bastard.

HUGO: Me lucky? Say, lady, ain't you hoid the one o'clock news? God is dead. And I'm not feeling so well myself. (*Their laughter echoes. They dance. YOUNG HUGO and YOUNG ADELE sit at the vacated table, pretend to be sophisticated. Smooching and drinking imaginary drinks, aping them, sending them up.*)

Adele, I need earthing. I need to make love to something. Is there a bagel shop in town?

ADELE: I'm going back to the hospital.

HUGO: Look! The hotel's come to us. Please!

ADELE: You're not human. Not nice.

HUGO: The troubles of this world are caused by nice people. Why am I so desperate tonight?

ADELE: So, tell me. Out with it?

HUGO: Out with it? In the street?

ADELE: What's really caused all this angst? Apart from Germany? Hugo! The truth.

HUGO: I didn't leave Sylvie. She left me.

ADELE: I know.

HUGO: What? You women. You're all chums together. You converse, conspire behind our back.

ADELE: Anyway, you're free. Isn't that what you wanted?

HUGO: But I wanted to be the one to leave.

ADELE: Men!

HUGO: He's more than twenty years younger!

ADELE: Lucky her.

HUGO: Sylvie made me.

ADELE: Made you do what?

HUGO: And now she's done this.

ADELE: (*Looking at her watch.*) I really must go. But thank you.

HUGO: For what?

ADELE: Understanding.

HUGO: I understand nothing.

ADELE: Well, thank you for being there.

HUGO: There? Where's there?

ADELE: Hugo! Hugo! Please think of me. And please pray. Goodbye.

HUGO: Pray? I wouldn't give God the snot from my nose. (*He calls.*) Adele! Don't... leave... (*But she has gone.*) Adele!

(*His voice echoes. He wanders towards YOUNG HUGO and YOUNG ADELE. The figures in the wine bar transform. The WAITRESS becomes KLARA, another figure his mother. MRS BAUER approaches him.*)

MRS BAUER: You drink at a time like this? (*No reply.*) Kurt!

(*HUGO becomes his father. But reality is slipping away and everyone seems sozzled. Grotesque figures out of a pre-war, expressionist Berlin painting.*)

HUGO: (*As Mr Bauer.*) I need to drink at a time like this. Up yours?

MRS BAUER: What?

HUGO: (*As Mr Bauer.*) Open your legs, for once in your life. Open your legs, woman. Is it still there?

MRS BAUER: If you could rise to the occasion.

HUGO: (*As Mr Bauer. Thrusts his hand up her skirt.*) Yes! It's still there. They haven't rationed it yet.

MRS BAUER: Kurt!

(*HUGO forces her down on the table, opens her legs wide then lies on top of her.*)

Kurt! Kurt!

HUGO: (*As Mr Bauer.*) Fucking makes free.

MRS BAUER: Kurt! The children! The children!

HUGO: (*As Mr Bauer.*) Leeds makes me randy.

MRS BAUER: Leeds? Kurt. What are you gibbering on about? Pull yourself together. It cannot be Klara.

HUGO: (*As Mr Bauer. Suddenly correct.*) No. It cannot be Klara.

MRS BAUER: Klara is far too frail.

HUGO: (*As Mr Bauer.*) Klara is far too frail.

MRS BAUER: And Rudi is far too young.

HUGO: (*As Mr Bauer.*) And Rudi is far too young.

MRS BAUER: You're right.

HUGO: (*As Mr Bauer.*) Am I?

MRS BAUER: Yes. Hugo is the right age. It must be Hugo.

HUGO: (*As Mr Bauer.*) It must be Hugo.

KLARA: Don't let him go.

YOUNG HUGO: I prefer to die with you than live without you.

MRS BAUER: Darling. What's this talk of dying? We're not going to die. Who said we are going to die?

KLARA: A family must stay together.

MRS BAUER: This invidious choice. This is their worst crime. It must be Hugo. Hugo is so gifted. My love, aren't you the lucky one? To be chosen.

HUGO: (*As Mr Bauer.*) Hugo! You are the one. You are the lucky one.

YOUNG HUGO: Bastard! I refuse to be chosen.

HUGO: (*As Mr Bauer.*) It's all been decided.

YOUNG HUGO: I refuse to be chosen. I hate you. Hate you. Mother! Save me. Please don't let him send me away. Save me! Save me!

(*She is helpless. YOUNG HUGO shakes with fury. The crowd from the wine bar become the HATE BRIGADE.*)

YOUNG HUGO: (*Pointing his finger at his father.*) You! You!

HUGO: (*As Mr Bauer. Commanding him to stop his fury.*) Boy! Boy!

YOUNG HUGO: You! You!

(*The watching mob mis-hear his words and slowly start to encircle HUGO and YOUNG HUGO.*)

HATE BRIGADE:(*Quietly at first, but building to a crescendo.*) Jew! Jew! Boy! Boy! Jew boy! Jew boy! Jew boy! Jew boy!

(*YOUNG HUGO now gets caught up in the hate and joins in with the others, enjoys screaming at his father.*)

YOUNG HUGO: Jew boy! Jew boy! Jew boy! Jew boy!

(*HUGO as Mr Bauer stands with his wife and daughter, withering in the centre of the mob. Now the mob melt away. YOUNG HUGO is quiet now.*)

I am not going.

(*The figures reassemble in the Leeds wine bar. They stand in a circle, silently kicking someone crouching on the ground. It is YOUNG HUGO. HUGO, no longer his father, is slumped on the table, drunk.*)

HUGO: I refuse to be chosen. I refuse to be chosen.

HATE BRIGADE:Jew boy! Jew boy! Jew boy! (*Then they turn and look ominously at HUGO.*)

HUGO: I refuse to be the chosen.

(*A bed appears. It seems suspended in the air. HUGO climbs onto it. A WAITER enters with a bottle of scotch. When the WAITER departs, HUGO immediately pours himself a drink.*)

The very first train out of this place. (*Consults a small timetable.*) Good! (*Turns on the radio and Glenn Miller's 'In the Mood' blares out.*) Where is he? Hugo? You still there? No? Sensible. I scare the living daylights out of ghosts. (*Snaps his fingers and YOUNG HUGO appears, handing HUGO his violin.*)

I intend to live an ordinary, quiet life, after this.

YOUNG HUGO: Where's Adele?

HUGO: Busy with her bag of bones. Inconsiderate bitch. Why doesn't he just get it over with?

YOUNG HUGO: All husbands seem to be dying these days.

HUGO: And all women are beyond me.

YOUNG HUGO: They know you too well.

HUGO: Sylvie steered me through life. Forty years. She taught me how to make people like me. Arranged everything. My programmes, my gestures. My responses. The clothes I wore. The style of my hair. Everything. She kept the monsters at bay. They'll tear me to pieces now.

YOUNG HUGO: Go to bed.

HUGO: Thank you. How kind. I'm there.

(*HUGO lies on the bed. Snaps his fingers. The wine bar dissolves and the Yorkshire countryside appears. YOUNG HUGO shakes a tree. YOUNG ADELE comes tumbling down, and falls on him. They roll over and over, cuddling, laughing.*)

YOUNG ADELE: 'Then all the worms will eat thee oop,
On Ilkley moor ba tat – then all the worms will eat thee,
then all the worms will eat thee…'
(*YOUNG HUGO joins her in the song. HUGO snores in his sleep.*)
(*Impersonating her older self.*) Hugo! Hold me. Hold me.
(*He does.*)
Hold me. Just hold me. Just love me.

YOUNG HUGO: (*Taking up the game.*) I love you. I shall love you forever.

YOUNG ADELE: And I will love you for ever and ever.
(*They kiss and continue the game.*)
Can you get it up?

YOUNG HUGO: How long have you got?

YOUNG ADELE: Half an hour.

YOUNG HUGO: Good. Time enough for a quickie.

YOUNG ADELE: When the prick stands the brain dies.

YOUNG HUGO: Roll on, brain death. Look! A blue butterfly. Quick!

YOUNG ADELE: No! Catch me.
(*She runs away, laughing. He chases her, grabs her. They roll over and over in long grass. Then silently they lie on their backs.*)

YOUNG HUGO: I love Yorkshire. This countryside. One day I'm going to bring Klara here.

YOUNG ADELE: Hugo is a really lovely name.

YOUNG HUGO: Those charcoal clouds, up there. They are people. See? That long hair. That's Klara, my sister. One day I shall see them all again.

YOUNG ADELE: No, you won't.

YOUNG HUGO: (*Not listening.*) Our two families can meet in Berlin. We'll all have a picnic.

YOUNG ADELE: Please hold me, Hugo.

YOUNG HUGO: You'll love Klara. And Rudi. Let's get back.

YOUNG ADELE: Where?

YOUNG HUGO: The future.

YOUNG ADELE: Shit.
(*They return to the hotel bedroom. HUGO is asleep on the bed. No one else is there. The kids drape themselves in blankets.*)

YOUNG HUGO: I am the sheik of Araby. And you are my slave girl.

143

YOUNG ADELE: Like hell. I am your queen. Bow down to me. (*He does. MRS BAUER appears.*)

MRS BAUER: The menorah. Where is it? (*YOUNG HUGO goes to the suitcase. Takes out the menorah. Holds it up.*)

Good. Never forget it, Hugo. Take it everywhere. Hold it high, well above everything. The cries. The flames. The smoke. It's the symbol of our faith. To remind us that life is mightier than death, and in the end this ridiculous hatred we all have for one another will disappear forever from the face of this earth.

HUGO: (*Mumbles.*) Mother… (*But she is gone.*)

YOUNG ADELE: Let's trick him.

YOUNG HUGO: Yes.

(*They stuff pillows onto the bed beside HUGO, and cover these with blankets. This is shaped to resemble a human form. They believe HUGO is still asleep, but he is now awake and wise to their tricks.*)

HUGO: (*Sitting up and seeing the shape. Acting.*) Why? What's this? Who's been sleeping in my porridge? Who have we here? Who can it be? (*Pulls back the blankets. But he is utterly astonished to see ADELE.*) Adele!

ADELE: I don't know. I hear from you once in a blue moon. You deign to phone me out of the blue. You lift me out of oblivion every so often. I'm your little bit of under in Leeds. You bastard. How convenient. I should have more pride. But I had to come.

HUGO: How?

ADELE: I managed.

HUGO: I only just left you.

ADELE: Hugo! It's two o'clock in the morning.

HUGO: Is he – ?

ADELE: Don't even talk about it. Here I am.

(*YOUNG HUGO sits in the corner, plays from 'Lark Ascending'. YOUNG ADELE wanders back into the wardrobe.*)

HUGO: I am so pleased to see you.

ADELE: Be nice to yourself, they said. Nothing you can do here. Go home. He's not going to die in the night.

HUGO: Take off your clothes.

ADELE: No.

HUGO: I'll undress you. (*He does.*)

ADELE: Monster. Why do I have even a modicum of desire for you? And at this moment of all times? I can't be long.

HUGO: Belong to me.

ADELE: Half an hour at the most. I must be home in case they ring.

HUGO: Be nice to yourself. We're only human.

ADELE: Hold me, Hugo. Please. Don't let me break down. Don't let me fall to pieces.

HUGO: It's my breakdown that stops me falling to pieces. You'll be alright. You're with me.

ADELE: This is the most terrible sin. Doing this and my husband, my darling husband, dying.

HUGO: Treachery and lovemaking are bedmates.
   (*They make love. YOUNG HUGO quickly goes to the wardrobe and pulls YOUNG ADELE out. They go to the bed to watch.*)

YOUNG ADELE: Don't they look funny doing that?

HUGO: How dare you? Get lost.

YOUNG HUGO: Sorry.
   (*He and YOUNG ADELE move away.*)
   All people look funny doing it. Except to themselves.

YOUNG ADELE: They're far too old.

YOUNG HUGO: Far, far too old. Shall we try it?

YOUNG ADELE: Maybe when I'm fourteen and a half.

ADELE: (*Sitting up.*) You haven't lost your touch. You play me like a violin. (*She stiffens when the phone rings, shattering the night.*)

HUGO: Stay there. Please. (*He answers the phone. Whispers.*) David? This time of night... What's wrong?... No... Listen! I can't talk now. Phone you back soon. (*Puts the phone down.*)

ADELE: Who was that?

HUGO: My son, the wine merchant.

ADELE: David? What did he want?

HUGO: What do they ever want? When they get in touch it's never to your benefit.
   (*ADELE gets out of bed.*)
   Can't you stay till morning?

ADELE: No. I shouldn't be here at all. I feel so guilty. (*Puts on his dressing gown.*) May I take a shower? (*Goes.*)
(*HUGO lifts the phone again.*)

HUGO: Reception? Get me London: 020 74550021.
(*Someone answers.*)
David!... You heard from Simon?... What?... Where is he?... That girl... Lotte. That German bitch? He phoned from Berlin... What? I don't believe it... (*Slumps into a chair.*) If nothing else has finished me, this has. It's the worst news I could have heard... David! Just keep the press away from me, for God's sake... I've got enough on my plate. I'm devastated. How could my own grandson do this to me?... Why? Why? How could he even think of marrying one of them? This is the final nail... Yes. Tomorrow morning... Goodnight.
(*Puts the phone down. YOUNG HUGO and YOUNG ADELE cuddle in their sleep.*)

ADELE: (*Emerging.*) That's better.

HUGO: (*Cheerfully embracing her.*) You know, for a grandmother you're really hot stuff.

ADELE: So what was that phone call all about?

HUGO: Nothing.

ADELE: You phoned him back.

HUGO: Yes.

ADELE: (*Remembering her husband.*) Is everything alright?

HUGO: Everything is absolutely hunky-dory.

ADELE: Good. (*She gets dressed.*)

HUGO: Stay with me. Let's watch the dawn coming up over Leeds.

ADELE: Please? May I? (*Indicates the phone.*)
(*HUGO nods.*)
(*ADELE makes a quick, whispered phone call.*)
Alright. I'm sure he'll be alright.
(*They both sit by the window as the sky slowly lightens.*)

HUGO: Breakfast! Let's have a feast. (*Into phone.*) Room 328. Can I order breakfast, for two?... I know it's very early... Sorry. (*To ADELE.*) English hotels! (*Into phone.*) Certainly. The customer is always wrong... Thank you...

That's awfully kind of you… Yes. Eggs, bacon, and some mushrooms and tomato and sausages and fried bread and toast. And marmalade… Yes. Something light. Thank you. Oh, yes. Send me up a morning paper… The *Guardian,* please… Thank you. And the *Daily Mail…* Forgive me. How kind. How very kind. (*To ADELE.*) You have to grovel.

(*YOUNG HUGO and YOUNG ADELE wake and stretch. The family sit in a circle. YOUNG HUGO gets his violin, plays Mozart. ADELE looks through HUGO's suitcase, takes out the menorah.*)

ADELE: What's this?

HUGO: Nothing.

ADELE: Your mother.

HUGO: Yes. Just something. No significance.

(*ADELE finds a travelling iron in his case and starts to press his suit. Time passes. A knock on the door. A WAITER is there with breakfast.*)

Breakfast is served, I believe. If I had to choose between Mozart and breakfast – no contest. Breakfast every time.

(*HUGO reads newspapers as ADELE sets the meal out on the table.*)

More riots. More deaths. We are numbed by overkill. Nothing touches us any more. News is created to deaden the mind. To close us down. To dehumanise us.

(*A police car rushes urgently somewhere. YOUNG HUGO and YOUNG ADELE come to the table and look longingly at the food, and nibble from the plates as HUGO and ADELE read the papers.*)

We are all consumers, customers. We are all the cost-effective generation now. Society? What did the blue angel of death say? What is society? Compassion is buried somewhere beneath the silt of greed and indifference. This is the age of acquiescence.

(*YOUNG HUGO and YOUNG ADELE now sit under the table. HUGO throws them food.*)

Kosher bacon! Superb! What could be nicer?

(*ADELE laughs. HUGO looks hurt.*)

ADELE: You've been pulling that joke for thirty years.

HUGO: Can you hear something? Someone crying?

(*A whisper of people crying and shouting far away.*)

ADELE: Seagulls. (*She gets up and puts on her coat.*)

HUGO: Seagulls over Leeds? What about us?

ADELE: I can't talk about that now.

(*They embrace. YOUNG HUGO and YOUNG ADELE fall upon the food.*)

HUGO: Adele! A hammer blow. My son the wine merchant informed me that... that Simon, my golden boy. My grandson... He's... I tell you, my family is out to get me. One way or another.

ADELE: What's he done?

HUGO: I hate them all.

ADELE: What about Simon?

HUGO: He's run away, to Germany. And if that is not enough he's gone after a girl he met at medical school. I told you about her. A little, titless, German bitch called Lotte? Apparently they're getting married. My grandson is getting married to Germany. It's the end of everything.

ADELE: Look. I have more terrible things to attend to.

HUGO: Don't you understand? Didn't you hear me?

ADELE: I heard you.

HUGO: Nothing's changed.

ADELE: Hugo! Face the future.

HUGO: I'm facing it. The future goes round and round, and it comes out here. Leading all the way back to the past. How can I betray them?

ADELE: What about the decoration?

HUGO: What decoration?

ADELE: The Knight Commander of Germany. You are going of course? Good. Goodbye. See you in the pass of coursing time. Phone me sometime. No. I'll contact you.

HUGO: I will not go. I cannot go. It's absurd. How dare they?

ADELE: Hugo! Get that bloody holocaust off your back! It gives you a stoop.

HUGO: Goodbye, Adele. Keep in touch. I hope he doesn't die.

ADELE: He will. Probably today. Or tomorrow. Thank you. Goodbye Hugo.

HUGO: Adele! I really appreciate you.

ADELE: Thanks. (*Goes.*)

(*HUGO seems crushed. YOUNG ADELE pours him a drink. She smiles sweetly.*)

HUGO: You know, Hugo, the dead don't get older. Your sister Klara is stuck at fourteen. She should be well into her late sixties now.

(*The HATE BRIGADE creep out of the wardrobe, come down front to confront and threaten the audience with deafening slogans.*)

HATE BRIGADE: *Sieg heil! Sieg heil!* Wogs out! Nignogs out! Pakis out! Yids out! Gas the lot! Gas the lot! Out! Out, out! England for the English! England for the English! *Sieg heil! Sieg heil! Sieg heil! Sieg heil! Sieg heil! Sieg heil!*

HUGO: (*Covers his ears.*) All my life I imagine this same mob.

HATE BRIGADE: *Sieg heil! Sieg heil!* Keep Britain white! Out with the niggers! Out with the Yids! Out with the Pakis! *Sieg heil! Sieg heil! Sieg heil!*

HUGO: What time is it?

YOUNG ADELE: Seven in the evening.

HUGO: But we just had breakfast.

YOUNG ADELE: They serve breakfast all day.

HUGO: And even now the same poison seeps out of the sewers. Klara was burned. Nothing was learned.

(*The HATE BRIGADE surround him.*)

HATE BRIGADE: Jew boy! Jew boy! Jew boy!

(*YOUNG HUGO and YOUNG ADELE are attracted to the mob and now get carried away and enjoy joining in.*)

Jew boy! Jew boy! Jew boy!

(*They seep back into the wardrobe.*)

HUGO: If I do nothing – nothing will change. If I do something... nothing will change. I'll do something.

(*YOUNG HUGO approaches him. He strokes his head.*)

YOUNG HUGO: You remind me of a man.

HUGO: What man?

YOUNG HUGO: The man with the power.

HUGO: What power?

YOUNG HUGO: The power of the hoodoo.

HUGO: Who do?

YOUNG HUGO: You do.

HUGO: I do what?

YOUNG HUGO: You remind me of a man. (*He hands HUGO the violin.*)

HUGO: I've lost the gift.

YOUNG HUGO: Try.

HUGO: I'll make a fool of myself.

YOUNG HUGO: It's all in the mind. Play!

HUGO: (*As he speaks he starts to pack his suitcase.*) A rabbi comes face to face with a cripple. 'Stand up straight!' the rabbi intones, in his deep voice. 'Throw away your crutches. I have spoken.' 'Don't be silly,' the cripple replies. 'If I throw away my crutches, I'll fall over.' 'Silence! Have faith. I have spoken. Throw away your crutches. You will not fall over.' 'Rabbi! I can't! I'm a cripple. If I throw away my crutches I'll fall over.' 'Silence! Have faith! I have spoken! You will not fall over! Throw away your crutches!'

YOUNG HUGO: So? What happened?

HUGO: The cripple threw away his crutches.

YOUNG HUGO: And?

HUGO: He fell over. (*They both laugh.*) If I am not a violinist I am nothing.

YOUNG HUGO: Play! Mr Nothing.

(*HUGO smiles, shakes his head and clasps his hands around YOUNG HUGO's throat, as if he were about to throttle him. YOUNG HUGO nods at the violin.*)

HUGO: Alright! Mr Slave-Driver.

(*YOUNG HUGO starts to play his violin and HUGO immediately takes up his violin, to play perfectly from the Mendelssohn violin concerto.*)

YOUNG HUGO: Easy. Piece of cake.

HUGO: If you are in harmony with yourself. (*Satisfied, he carries YOUNG HUGO back to the wardrobe.*) Now stay dead. (*Then to YOUNG ADELE.*) You as well.

(*YOUNG ADELE joins YOUNG HUGO in the wardrobe. But YOUNG HUGO quickly looks out to throw a smile to HUGO.*)

YOUNG HUGO: Catch!

HUGO: (*Collecting the smile.*) Thank you. (*He sings 'In the Mood' quietly. He has packed. Now he puts the violin into its case, grabs the menorah and makes for the door.*) I'm going to Germany. (*Exits.*)

(*YOUNG HUGO laughs, then closes the wardrobe door upon himself.*)

End of Act One.

ACT TWO

A hotel room. Berlin. Morning. HUGO is just finishing shaving. He sprays some cologne on his face then goes to the wardrobe. Opens it.

HUGO: Alright. You can come out.

YOUNG HUGO: I was having a lovely dream. You spoilt it.

HUGO: We're expecting someone.

YOUNG HUGO: (*Emerging.*) I'm hungry.

HUGO: So, what's new? How about some knackwurst and sauerkraut? (*He picks up the phone.*)

YOUNG HUGO: Forget it. Why did you bring me here?

HUGO: (*Tunes his violin.*) Look out of the window. I've exorcised all my darkest fears. It's a human, thriving city. The young look healthy, sane. Human. So? What are we waiting for?

YOUNG HUGO: No problem.

(Takes up his violin and therefore HUGO is able to play from Sibelius, quite beautifully. Then HUGO stops, drinks from a full glass.)

Whisky? This time of day?

(The phone rings.)

HUGO: Young Hugo, get lost.

(YOUNG HUGO blows a raspberry, then goes to a corner.)

But don't let me down.

YOUNG HUGO: Your command is my wish.

HUGO: (*Answering the phone.*) Send her up. (*He opens the main door slightly, takes up his violin.*) Come, my old darling. Let us impress her. 'Deep in the forest. *Tif in Vedele.*' The dead need a proper lullaby.

(He and YOUNG HUGO play the Yiddish song. The YOUNG WOMAN enters. HUGO knows she is there but plays on. Then he abruptly stops to greet her.)

Fraulein. How nice. Please sit down.

YOUNG WOMAN: You were just playing something so beautiful. It was so moving.

HUGO: It is a Yiddish folk song. A dead song of a dead people. You have such amazing eyes.

YOUNG WOMAN: Thank you. The violin is not like any other instrument. It is as if the gods gave it as a gift to humans. Do you agree?

HUGO: Of course. Maybe you would like to touch her.

YOUNG WOMAN: Her? You see the violin as woman?

HUGO: Please! I couldn't be that banal. This is my holy of holies. (*Hands her the violin.*)

YOUNG WOMAN: *(Holding it as if she were cradling a baby.)* I must be careful. It is so precious. Is it – she, very old?

HUGO: Very, very old. She was created by Signor Giuseppe Guarnieri del Gesu, of Cremona. If she were not so valuable I would contemplate having her buried with me. She is not to be understood. A mixture of pure simplicity and great complexity. She has seen it all. Knows everything. Witnessed all the madness of Europe, for more than two hundred and fifty years. Yet, she still sings. Isn't that amazing? The secret is in the wood. The wood must be sound and handsome. This wood is the finest. From across the Adriatic. And do remember the obsessive care that goes into the varnish. Her overcoat. Now, young lady, you are from… Ah yes, the *Frankfurter Allgemeiner*. What can I do you for? Are you comfortable?

YOUNG WOMAN: Thank you, sir. I am privileged that you have granted me this interview.

HUGO: My pleasure. Do you have any Jewish blood by any chance?

YOUNG WOMAN: Why? Do you need a transfusion? (*He laughs.*) Sorry. I couldn't resist the joke. It was impertinent of me.

HUGO: I thought it was very funny. How nice that you don't come at me with the usual awe. You make me feel quite human. Seriously, you do look somewhat Hebraic.

YOUNG WOMAN: Really? How romantic.

HUGO: Would you like some whisky?

YOUNG WOMAN: (*Refusing.*) Thank you. Never when I'm working. (*HUGO refills his glass, drinks more.*)

HUGO: It's those eyes. So deep, so sad. So Jewish.

153

YOUNG WOMAN: I'm afraid the truth is far more mundane. My family are from Hamburg. Far, far into the distance.

HUGO: Hamburg shines in my dark memory. It was the one city that Hitler refused to visit.

YOUNG WOMAN: Thank you.

HUGO: You have perhaps a tinge of Italian blood?

YOUNG WOMAN: We are German through and through, I'm afraid. Chance has made us what we are. Mr Bauer, the questions.

HUGO: Sorry. Shoot.

(*Switches on a small recorder.*)

YOUNG WOMAN: Mr Hugo Bauer, how do you feel returning to Germany after all these years?

HUGO: I feel great. There's a vivacity, a great energy here. I feel quite at home. Of course, memories flood back but I'm glad I've returned at last.

YOUNG WOMAN: And how do you feel about the honour to be bestowed upon you tonight? The highest decoration that the state can award?

HUGO: What can I say? I feel it probably the most important thing that ever happened to me. I am deeply, deeply moved.

YOUNG WOMAN: Yet you made a statement, eighteen months ago when you were interviewed by the *Guardian* newspaper in London. I quote: 'The wall may be down but my wall is never down... Only when the last German roasts in hell...'

(*HUGO drinks more.*)

HUGO: I know what I said. I was upset at the time. I was ill. I once had a negative attitude to this nation. Understandably. But now I want to close the door to the past. It's no good hating all your life. It poisons you. This decoration means that the past has been wiped clean. It draws a line... I feel we are entering a new era... Oh! What shice! (*Turns off the tape recorder. Drinks more.*) My family were all gassed and hosed away. And I survived. I was chosen. They had to die. Once. I have to relive their deaths over and over again. My home, my childhood was wrenched from me by the good citizens of this land. Do you want to know the real reason why I came to this... place? My grandson ran off with a German girl, a *Tochter* of Elysium. Simon is marrying Lotte. Isn't that sweet? Shake hands, we're all related now. Now my blood and your blood will flow into each other. (*He laughs too much.*)

YOUNG WOMAN: I'm sorry. I shall go now.

HUGO: Not your fault. What's your name?

YOUNG WOMAN: Marguerite.

HUGO: You've got beautiful hair. Shall I play for you?

YOUNG WOMAN: Unfortunately I must go now.

HUGO: Stay. Talk to me. I'm feeling displaced. Lost. Are you really there? (*Goes towards her.*) Let me touch you. To prove you exist.
(*Places his hand on her breast. She freezes.*)

YOUNG WOMAN: No.

HUGO: Fraulein! Please. Why are you so afraid of me? (*Puts his arm around her.*) Come. You are cold.
(*She draws away.*)

YOUNG WOMAN: I must go.

HUGO: Do you have many boyfriends? I can see you are not only compassionate, but very passionate.

YOUNG WOMAN: Did you hate your mother so much?

HUGO: I don't understand.

YOUNG WOMAN: You may be a genius. But you have a lack of respect for a respectable man.

HUGO: What did you say before that?

YOUNG WOMAN: I said 'Did you hate your mother so much?'

HUGO: What did you mean?

YOUNG WOMAN: Work it out for yourself. I think you know, deep down.

HUGO: How dare you! Get out!

YOUNG WOMAN: I think you need some sleep, Herr Bauer.

HUGO: Yes. The sleep you gave, tried to give us all. Please go! Out, you silly, little bitch. (*Then, pulling himself together, he takes up the violin and again plays the Yiddish melody.*)

YOUNG WOMAN: You play like a god, yet you behave like a silly child.

HUGO: Fraulein, I think you misunderstood my intentions. Goodnight.

YOUNG WOMAN: Goodnight, Mr Bauer.

HUGO: Perhaps we can meet in a café tomorrow? You could do the interview then?

YOUNG WOMAN: Perhaps. Goodbye. (*Goes.*)

HUGO: (*Slams a pillow at the door.*) German bitch! (*Laughs.*) Did I hate my mother? What did she think? That I wanted to get into her Nazi knickers? How could I hope to survive the scandal? (*Drinks. Lifts the phone.*) Reception?… I want Great Britain… Yes. Leeds… I can. What's the code?… (*Jots down the information.*) Thank you. (*Starts to dial but then changes his mind, sits in an armchair.*) Too tired. The pain. Let it all come. (*Drinks and slumps into a sleep.*)

(*YOUNG HUGO goes to the wardrobe, opens it and takes out the luggage he had when he left Berlin in 1939. Then he whistles into the wardrobe. YOUNG ADELE gingerly emerges from the dark. She too has luggage. The young people slowly walk into 1939. It is as if the sleeping HUGO is dreaming this.*)

YOUNG HUGO: Leeds, 1939. Hugo? Remember?

(*HUGO grunts in his sleep. A row of houses and two adult figures emerge from the wardrobe. We have seen them before. They become MR and MRS LEVY, but younger now. They sit in the living room of their house. He starts knitting, she smokes a pipe and reads a newspaper. YOUNG HUGO and YOUNG ADELE approach.*)

YOUNG ADELE: (*Singing.*) 'Hitler! He's only got one ball. Goering has two but rather small. Himmler is somewhat sim'lar. And Herr Goebbels has no balls at all.'

YOUNG HUGO: I'm staying with a (*Consulting a note.*) Doctor and Mrs Levy.

YOUNG ADELE: And I'm staying with Mr and Mrs Conway.

YOUNG HUGO: (*Shaking hands formally.*) Goodbye, Adele.

YOUNG ADELE: Goodbye, Hugo.

YOUNG HUGO: I wish you luck.

YOUNG ADELE: I'll need it.

YOUNG HUGO: Kiss me.

YOUNG ADELE: No. Oh, alright. (*Closes her eyes and pouts her lips.*)

(*YOUNG HUGO cups her breasts and kisses her.*)

YOUNG HUGO: (*Laughing.*) 'Rosy apple lemonade tart, tell me the name of your sweetheart.'

YOUNG ADELE: You're a terrible boy. (*Re-enters the wardrobe.*)

YOUNG HUGO: (*Sits outside the house, writing an invisible letter.*) Dear Mother and Father. Rudi. Klara.

(*They appear.*)

I have just arrived in Leeds but my heart and mind are in Germany. Leeds is very nice and quiet and the people are kind. So I don't always feel homesick. But I miss Germany. The ice cream. School. You are probably all together now at a picnic. It's midsummer. But where am I? You're all there without me. If you are going to die, I would rather die with you than live without you. Mother, don't worry about me. I'm fine and healthy. I remember us all laughing. Laughing. And here I am. Remember last summer.

(*His family assemble at a picnic. They laugh and eat as Django Reinhardt and the Hot Club de Paris play jazz music. KLARA is suddenly there.*)

Klara!

(*KLARA gets up, starts dancing. The others join in.*)

I'm sending this letter to our home. Are you still there? I expect so. I'm addressing it there. But if not… if not… where are you? I'm not even sure this letter will ever reach you. (*He concludes with head in hands.*) Can they ever forgive me for sending me away?

(*Knocks on the door of the Levy house. They open and take him inside. HUGO gets out of his hotel armchair and also enters the house. MR LEVY takes YOUNG HUGO's case. But YOUNG HUGO refuses to part with his violin. The picnic in Berlin continues.*)

MRS LEVY: You play the violin?

YOUNG HUGO: A little.

MRS LEVY: How nice. You must play for us one day.

YOUNG HUGO: How kind.

MR LEVY: We've been looking forward to this, haven't we, Muriel?

MRS LEVY: Yes, Maurice.

YOUNG HUGO: Where are your children?

MRS LEVY: We haven't any. (*Silence.*) I'll get some tea.

MR LEVY: How kind.

(*MRS LEVY goes. MR LEVY lays the table.*)

YOUNG HUGO: Why do you not have any paintings on the wall?

MR LEVY: Leeds is a very interesting, very historic city.

YOUNG HUGO: Do you go to concerts?

MR LEVY: Leeds is situated in West Riding of Yorkshire. The population of Leeds is 494,000 souls. The census was last year.

YOUNG HUGO: My father is probably the best architect in all Germany.

MR LEVY: Leeds is a very interesting, very historic city. Leeds or, if you like, Loidis or Ledes belonged to the kingdom of Elmete and was ruled by British chieftains until Edwin conquered Northumbria in the seventh century.

YOUNG HUGO: (*Yawns.*) How kind.

MR LEVY: I hope I am not boring you.

YOUNG HUGO: You are as a matter of fact.

MR LEVY: Would you like to wash your hands before tea?

YOUNG HUGO: How kind. But I am not unclean.

(*MRS LEVY returns with tea.*)

MRS LEVY: Toasted muffins. And try some of that delicious strawberry jam.

YOUNG HUGO: How kind.

MRS LEVY: Then I expect you want to rest. We've got the room all nicely ready for you.

YOUNG HUGO: How kind.

MR LEVY: I think we are going to have some really jolly times together.

MRS LEVY: Wouldn't that be nice?

YOUNG HUGO: How kind. (*They sit and eat silently.*)

MR LEVY: It's raining. Funny. It comes straight through the ceiling.

(*It is raining in the living room. And in Berlin. HUGO's family in Germany quickly finish their picnic.*)

YOUNG HUGO: Goodbye, Klara!

(*MRS LEVY looks perturbed.*)

HUGO: My sister.

KLARA: Goodbye, Hugo. (*She hurries after the others who return to the wardrobe.*)

YOUNG HUGO: Klara!

(*YOUNG HUGO gets up from the table, goes upstairs, finds himself in his bedroom that is already being explored by HUGO. YOUNG HUGO unpacks. Puts the menorah on the mantlepiece, then takes up the violin. HUGO studies the way YOUNG HUGO holds the instrument, and corrects the positioning, slightly. YOUNG HUGO, however, is overcome and sits on the bed, holding back tears. HUGO returns the violin to the reluctant YOUNG HUGO.*)

Who's haunting who?

HUGO: You remind me of a man.

YOUNG HUGO: Not playing.

HUGO: It's my turn now. You remind me of a man.

YOUNG HUGO: (*Reluctantly.*) What man?

HUGO: The man with the power?

YOUNG HUGO: What power?

HUGO: The power to be brave.

YOUNG HUGO: Who, me?

HUGO: Yes. You do.

YOUNG HUGO: I do what?

HUGO: You remind me of a man. Play.

YOUNG HUGO: Must I?

HUGO: This violin is your family now. It is the one thing that will hold you together. In here live your mother and father, sister and brother. You will never see them again but you will hear them laugh and cry in here. This is your home from now on. And you must practice survival, over and over and over again. How else will you keep them alive? Play!

(*YOUNG HUGO starts to play 'Lark Ascending'. MRS LEVY enters. At first he does not hear her, but then he suddenly stops playing, turns to her.*)

MRS LEVY: Oh. I hadn't realised. I thought it was a hobby.

(*YOUNG HUGO continues playing. MR LEVY comes.*)

MR LEVY: My God.

(*YOUNG HUGO stops playing.*)

They've sent us a bloody genius.

MRS LEVY: We must make sure we get him proper tuition. Maurice! The poor boy's dropping on his feet. Goodnight, Hugo.

YOUNG HUGO: Goodnight.

(*MRS LEVY goes towards him. He hesitates then cuddles in against her, trying to hide the fact that he is crying. Then he snaps.*)

Get out! Out! Out you... you... Bloody Jew... out! Out! Out!

MR LEVY: What? How dare...

MRS LEVY: Shush! Hugo!

YOUNG HUGO: Get out! I don't care any more. I don't care. I don't care.

(*MRS LEVY gestures to MR LEVY. HUGO rejects them from his memory. They return into the wardrobe.*)

HUGO: And so I settled in for the long night of Leeds death. Of nothingness.

(*YOUNG HUGO plays. HUGO, in the shadows, guides him.*)

No! Like this. Like this.

(*HUGO takes the violin to show YOUNG HUGO. Then he lies on the bed.*)

Tired. Endless repetition. Endless revision. Here I am, playing my life through over and over again.

YOUNG HUGO: Must try, or they will die. Keep in your head. Or they're all dead.

HUGO: Enough.

(*YOUNG HUGO continues.*)

I said you've done enough. Bed now. Sleep. You've done enough.

(*Lifts YOUNG HUGO up onto his shoulders and carries him back to the hotel room. YOUNG HUGO scuttles back into the wardrobe. HUGO lies on the bed.*)

Now I lay me down to sleep. I think I hear my parents weep. If I should die before I wake, it won't be soon enough. Wake me when the world turns over.

(*A siren sounds. Bombs fall. Explosions reverberate. Vera Lynn sings 'The White Cliffs of Dover'.*)

HUGO: And darkness covers the face of the earth. Behold, this dreamer cometh, surrounded and succoured by the cocoon of the whispering doctor of Roundhay, Leeds. And his creeping wife, Muriel, who feed me toasted muffins, and I hear every tick of the clock in that living room. Four years pass. There is no news of anything. Except the deaths of ships and sailors on the seas, and soldiers on battlefields and civilians in cities. But God is as silent as the Pope. Minutes drag seconds, slowly, but time speeds up until everyone falls off the earth, and years pass in a blink.

(*The all-clear sounds. YOUNG HUGO arises and plays from Berg's violin concerto. The hotel room is now bathed in daylight, but HUGO still sleeps in the bed. The blankets have fallen on the floor. A woman comes and covers him.*)

MRS BAUER: Never forget you're Jewish, no matter what the cost. Wrap up warm. Drink lots of milk. Find a nice girl. Fall in love. Don't kill yourself, because then we'll all be dead forever and no one will know that we were ever here.

HUGO: (*Quietly.*) Mother, it was you.

MRS BAUER: Me? What?

HUGO: It was you.

MRS BAUER: Hugo! What are you saying?

HUGO: (*Dismisses a not quite tangible thought from his mind.*) Sorry. Nothing. Mother. She's left me. Sylvie. My wife. I'm all alone. In the end we're all alone. Mother? You have no flesh. It's all been burnt away. You're smoke. You're nothing. You've got no face. So how can I dream you smelling warm, like this?

MRS BAUER: You awake?

HUGO: No.

MRS BAUER: Then go back to sleep. I'm not here.

HUGO: (*Waking.*) Mother! My life is dribbling away. I want to get on with it. What's left of it. Holocaust! Get off my

back. How can I live without my happy family mask?
Sylvie was my creator. I was her golem. She wove my
smiling mask, tuned my gentle soft voice; masterminded
my career, sewed the seams to cover the tears in my
soul. Now it's all coming apart. I can't live without her.

YOUNG HUGO: Really? Does Adele know this?

HUGO: Adele never meant anything to me. She knows
that. She knows the score. To hell with her. It's Sylvie.
I've got this physical pain, here in my stomach, when
I think of her. Imagine. Running off with a boy half
her age. I lay in bed beside her, for months and
months. Years. Unaware of his existence. Wrapped in
my ghosts, my past. My wonderful career. Meanwhile
he was knocking her off, five times a day. And I didn't
even notice the spring in her step. Her merriment.
The way she walked. Moved. She couldn't hide it from
the world. But she didn't have to hide it from me.
I didn't have an inkling; didn't notice the lovebites on
the inside of her thighs. She flaunted them before me
to make me burn with rage. I didn't even notice.

YOUNG HUGO: That was the biggest arrogance.

HUGO: She's dead. I've buried her, the bitch.

YOUNG HUGO: Hugo. This is not Leeds. The smells are
different. Where are we?

HUGO: Ah, know-all. You're lost for once in your death.
I'm in charge now. We are where it all happens.

YOUNG HUGO: I don't care where we are as long as you
order some food.

(*Now we clearly see the Berlin hotel bedroom. HUGO takes
up the phone. YOUNG HUGO departs.*)

HUGO: The operator said you can dial direct and get
straight through to Leeds. (*Takes out the piece of paper with
the scribbled number and dials.*) Adele?... How is he?...
Really?... Really? You have to hand it to him. The way
he clings... to life. I'm pleased. I'm praying for him.
(*Toasts the ceiling and drinks again.*) Adele!... I promise.
I haven't touched a drop. I'm off the stuff. I'm playing
tonight... Yes, I know I promised... I am coming back to
Leeds... Soon. Do me a small favour, please. Contact my

agents. Brenner and Caxton. Tell them to fix a firm date, within the next few weeks, if possible. They've got my diary. They know exactly what happened and I'm feeling terribly contrite. Tell them I'll fit it in, whenever it's convenient... Adele, bless you. You are most kind and you make so few demands. I feel so guilty... I'm not just using you. I have a deep, deep love and respect for you... Believe me... Yes. I'm in fine form... Imagine. Me becoming a Knight Commander of the Serene Republic of Germany... I'm having a wonderful time here... Germany is divine. Mystical. The views are wonderful. The Unter den Linden magnificent. The cafés sparkling. The cosmopolitan atmosphere. Kurt Weill and Herr Grosz sends their warmest regards... To be honest, Adele, I haven't stepped out of my hotel suite... Forgive me. If I didn't laugh I would cry... I'm thinking of you. You're a very brave girl... Please don't cry... Yes... Soon. Goodbye.

(*As soon as he puts the phone down it rings.*)

(*Answering it.*) ... I see. Thank you.

(*There is an immediate knocking on a door. He opens it but no one is there. The knocking persists. Then he opens the wardrobe. YOUNG HUGO crouches there.*)

Where else would you be?

(*He laughs gently. YOUNG HUGO emerges. Then HUGO sees the uncertain YOUNG ADELE within.*)

You as well?

(*YOUNG ADELE emerges. HUGO looks out of the window.*)

Berlin! So, I've returned to you?

YOUNG HUGO: We've been rehearsing. Come on, Adele. Show him.

(*YOUNG ADELE takes the stage in a childlike attempt at impersonating a sexy Marlene Dietrich singing 'Falling in Love Again'. The kids fall over, laughing.*)

YOUNG HUGO: So, what can I do you for?

HUGO: I need a face. Quick!

(*YOUNG HUGO quickly throws HUGO a smile. There is a knock on the door. SIMON, his grandson, stands there.*)

YOUNG HUGO sits, watching these entire proceedings. HUGO hugs SIMON for a time. They sway together, in silence.)

SIMON: Grandpa!

HUGO: Simon! Simon!

SIMON: Grandpa! You're crushing me.

HUGO: Let me take a look at you. (*Stands back, admiring.*)

SIMON: You look marvellous. Like a crazy Old Testament prophet.

HUGO: Simon, what do you want? Hang on, got a penknife? I'll cut my heart out for you.

SIMON: What does that mean?

HUGO: I don't know. I had it all planned. A diatribe. A dramatic confrontation. Old Testament curses, threats. But you in the flesh changes everything.

SIMON: Grandpa! You alright?

HUGO: I'm fine.

SIMON: You didn't come to Germany because of me, did you?

HUGO: No. What on earth do you mean? Haven't you heard my news? They want to decorate this illustrious clown, for his services to humanity.

SIMON: Decorate you? What with? Feathers?

HUGO: Feathers would be perfect. And tar. Sit down. (*SIMON doesn't comply.*)

SIMON: How's the fiddling?

HUGO: I've never fiddled better. I'm at the top of my form.

SIMON: I'm so proud of you.

HUGO: Didn't anyone tell you about my decoration?

SIMON: No. And didn't anyone tell you my news?

HUGO: News? What news?

SIMON: I thought you might have heard. Maybe they were afraid. I'm getting married. Today.

HUGO: What? Marvellous. My grandson getting married? To a girl?

SIMON: No. To a horse. Grandpa! I'm so delighted to see you. What a fortunate coincidence. Grandpa! You must come to the wedding. At least to the party. You'll be the only one from our family. Good. That's settled.

HUGO: Is it?

SIMON: Her name is Lotte. She's beautiful. We're having a picnic. On Lake Wannsee. You'll love her parents. Isn't it marvellous that the past's dead and buried?

HUGO: Yes. Dead and buried.

SIMON: How's Grandma?

HUGO: Wonderful. Simon, what about your future?

SIMON: Future?

HUGO: A Jew in Germany?

SIMON: What does that mean?

HUGO: Nothing.

SIMON: Grandpa, the past is dead. You must forgive.

HUGO: It is not within my power to forgive. That's God's job.

SIMON: There's only now. There's only us. There's only now. The future's too bleak to think about.

HUGO: Then let's stop thinking. Simon, I'm happy for you. I sang you lullabies. Come here.

SIMON: I haven't got much time.

HUGO: So, you've thrown up your studies.

SIMON: Grandpa! Look! (*Writes a quick note.*) Here! Time and place. You come to my ceremony and I promise to come to yours.

HUGO: Issa deal!

(*They shake hands and hug.*)

SIMON: Anyway, I would have made a terrible doctor. I don't know how to play God. The picnic is on Lake Wannsee. You know Lake Wannsee?

HUGO: (*Laughs.*) I know it well.

SIMON: You are my favourite ancestor, believe me.

HUGO: Simon, what's life all about?

SIMON: Life's all about getting through it. (*He goes to the door.*)

HUGO: Simon!

(*SIMON opens the door, he sees LOTTE outside.*)

SIMON: I didn't want you to come... (*But it's too late.*) Grandpa! I want you to meet...

(*LOTTE walks in. She easily could be KLARA, one of HUGO's ghosts.*)

Grandpa, this is Lotte.

HUGO: Klara!

(*For a moment LOTTE and HUGO just stare at each other. LOTTE radiates joy and beauty. She shakes hands with HUGO.*)

LOTTE: I have heard so much about you.

HUGO: I can see why he's bowled over. Look. Sorry. I'm so tired. I must rest.

LOTTE: I understand.

SIMON: Come on, Lotte. (*Leaves the room.*)

LOTTE: But you will come to our wedding?

HUGO: How could I refuse you? Lotte, you are most beautiful.

LOTTE: Oh, we Germans can be quite beautiful and human, occasionally. Mr Bauer, I try to understand the pain in your heart. But things have changed in this country. Many of us are fighting for a better world. We hate any form of racism. I want you to know I love Simon more than I love anyone.

HUGO: I believe you. I want to believe you.

SIMON: (*Off.*) Lotte!

LOTTE: Coming. (*On impulse she kisses HUGO.*) Goodbye. (*She goes.*)

HUGO: Oh God. (*He hides his face in his hands and sobs.*) Klara! Klara! What will hold me together, if I lose my hatred?

YOUNG HUGO: (*Emerging.*) It's tough.

HUGO: What's tough?

YOUNG HUGO: Life.

HUGO: What's life?

YOUNG HUGO: Life's a magazine.

HUGO: How much?

YOUNG HUGO: Ten cents.

HUGO: I haven't got ten cents.

YOUNG HUGO: It's tough. Let's go.

HUGO: Where?

YOUNG HUGO: All aboard. Adele. Quick. We're sailing. The bed is a boat. Adele!

YOUNG ADELE: (*Coming out of the wardrobe and jumping on the boat.*) Next stop! Lake Wannsee… Weeeeeeeeeeeeeeeeeee!

YOUNG HUGO: Hugo. We can't sail without you.

YOUNG ADELE: Lake Wannsee! Lake Wannsee! Weeeeee! (*HUGO jumps aboard and the bed sails. Lake Wannsee appears and waiting for them, amongst the other figures, are LOTTE's parents, the WEBERS.*)

SIMON: Lake Wannsee, Grandpa. We're there! Anything wrong?

HUGO: Nothing.

LOTTE: Oh, you must meet my parents.

HUGO: Delighted. Delighted. (*Shakes hands with them.*)

MR WEBER: Welcome to our wedding picnic on Lake Wannsee.

HUGO: Lake Wannsee. Such a beautiful setting. (*Hands the young people a wrapped present.*) Open it later. (*Hugs SIMON and then LOTTE.*) Klara!
(*Another figure approaches: an old man who is LOTTE's grandfather, PETER. He and HUGO stare at each other.*)

MRS WEBER: Oh, you must meet my father.

HUGO: (*Shaking hands with PETER.*) Delighted.

MRS WEBER: Forgive him. He's never quite with us, are you, Father?
(*PETER smiles.*)
Father, this is Hugo Bauer. *The* Hugo Bauer. I told you about him. Simon's grandfather.
(*PETER smiles and hugs HUGO. MRS WEBER hugs HUGO.*)
How wonderful. We are joined.

HUGO: Yes. Forgive and forget.
(*Everyone smiles.*)

MR WEBER: Thank you.

MRS WEBER: Simon is truly a wonderful boy.

HUGO: And your daughter lights up the world.
(*They all drink and eat. HUGO embraces SIMON and they quietly dance a gentle Jewish dance together. LOTTE joins them. Now the three dance together. Meanwhile LOTTE's parents dance a German dance.*)

MRS WEBER: Play for us, please.

MR WEBER: We would be deeply honoured.

HUGO: I was saving myself for the big event, tonight. You understand?

MRS WEBER: Yes. Of course we understand.

MR WEBER: How fortunate to be gifted. You must love your work.

HUGO: I hate music.

MR WEBER: Such delicious irony. Simon, your grandfather has a Berlin sense of humour.

HUGO: The joy gives me pain.

MRS WEBER: I understand.

LOTTE: But you will be wonderful tonight. I know.

HUGO: I hope. I'm actually thinking of giving it all up.

SIMON: Take no notice. He always carries on like this, before a concert. We've all got used to it.

HUGO: I seek ordinariness. True love.

MRS WEBER: Look no further. (*Referring to LOTTE and SIMON.*) We will have beautiful mixed, Jewish and German children, together. And we will love them.

HUGO: (*Disbelief.*) You believe that?

MRS WEBER: Of course.

MR WEBER: We are all human. All the same.

HUGO: I see, said the blind man.

MR WEBER: We will all live in beauty and peace.

HUGO: But will we live to see it?

MRS WEBER: What is happening on the streets of Germany at the moment is a passing phase. Dispossessed, lost youths. Not the real Germany.

MR WEBER: A minority, I assure you.

HUGO: Alright. I'm in the mood. Hugo! Let's swing.
(*HUGO and YOUNG HUGO play happy Jewish freilichs including 'Tum Balalaika'. They all dance together. HUGO dances beautifully with PETER, until they both fall down, happy and breathless. PETER is very drunk.*)

PETER: Give me a kiss. (*Pulling HUGO towards him, and kissing him.*)

HUGO: I can smell my people on you.

PETER: Marvellous. I love your people. The English.

HUGO: Your granddaughter is a beautiful girl.

PETER: Yes. As beautiful as her mother, my daughter. Thank God she takes after my side, the Koslovs.
(*The wind starts to howl and Mussorgsky's 'Songs and Dances of Death' plays. The people at the wedding feast dance in slow motion.*)

HUGO: Koslov? Ukrainian?

PETER: Exactly. Not a fucking German, thank you. I'm Peter. Hi there! Hi there! Dance with me, Kyrylo! Alexi! You fucking Russian pig. Why are you not dancing? Drink. Drink and dance. Kyrylo! I can see two of you. April 1941. We are trained by Nazis in preparation for the invasion of Russia. The best. I am almost twenty years old. July the second and third, 1941. We move into Lvov. Seven thousand… Point blank. The bullet sings. Sergei! You fucking cunt. Come, I want to kiss your ugly arse. Are you there? Are you really there? Dance. Just dance. You are commanded to dance. You must understand. We were the persecuted, not the persecutors. The Russians! They were the enemy. The Jews were nothing; sure, sure they exploited us, as usual. They came around, selling chickens door to door, putting poor farmers out of business, undercutting, overcharging.

HUGO: Both at the same time?

PETER: I hear you play the fiddle?

HUGO: A little.

PETER: I play the fiddle. Later we can fiddle together.

HUGO: *Wunderbar.*

PETER: Shall we join the others?

HUGO: July the second, 1941? You were saying?

PETER: Who will look after me when I am old? I beg my daughter. When I reach eighty, please creep up behind me and put a bullet through the back of my skull. No reply. Look! She smiles. Kids of today. No respect. Hi there! Hi there! Dance with me, Kyrylo! Alexi! You fucking Russian pig. Why are you not dancing? Drink. Drink and dance. Kyrylo! I can see two of you. Hey there! Hey there! Dance with me, Kyrylo. Kyrylo! I can see two of you. Are you there? Are you really there?

HUGO: What happened in Lvov?

PETER: Lvov?

HUGO: July the second and third, 1941. You moved into Lvov.

PETER: Father, forgive me for I have sinned. It has been many, many years since my last confession. Almost twenty. My sin was long ago. I have never talked about it to another living soul. Except Natalia. She's dead. Fuck her. There it is. Enter. Come with me into my childhood. This way. Careful. The cows are in the living room. Church in the bedroom. Bells in my father's head. Devil in his eyes. The Pope. Trees. Brides. Cocks. Drunken uncles. Idiot aunts. Down we go. Strikes. Famine. Poverty. Death. Wait! Must cut the balls off this bullock. That little Jew boy in the corner, him playing his fiddle.

(*YOUNG HUGO is there, playing the 'Partita' by Bach.*)

I last saw him in Lvov. I was one among millions.

HUGO: July, 1941! What happened ? You entered Lvov!

PETER: Down and down into a whirlwind. Father, the Church is our great protector. His Holiness Pope Pius XII understands how we need a bulwark against the red hoards, the Bolsheviks, our hated masters in Moscow. So we cheer them in. The Nazis. My mother, my father, my sisters and brothers cheer and wave our swastikas. They come as liberators. We are the oppressed, our land is occupied. My hatred for the Russians comes with mother's milk. We fight for the holy mother of God. They are recruiting units to fight against the Soviets. Codename 'Roland' and 'Nachtigall'. They come with brass bands. They have such beautiful uniforms. I am transformed in the mirror. My uniform brings me respect. I am someone. I am no longer a thin, underfed, starving, Ukrainian kid. People's eyes beg for favours. For mercy. Hey there! Hey there! Dance with me, Kyrylo. Sebastian! Why are you not dancing? Drink. Drink and dance. Kyrylo! I can see two of you. We advance into Galicia and the Western Ukraine. July the second, 1941. Hot day. Perfect. Not a whisp of cloud in the sky. We enter Lvov. The Jews. A clever people. A close, clannish people. I have nothing against them. Tenements. They stink. The SS man laughs. 'Now prove yourself! Little turnip!' I smash down doors. 'Everyone out! Out!' We put them to the torch. But they sing as they come out of the flames. Silence. No one cries. Crouching with his arms half-raised is this child, as if pulling down the sky, his imminent destination. But he is different; not like the others. He comes out smiling. 'You! Little Yid! Why are you smiling?' 'Koslov! Teach the little bastard a lesson. Show them what we do to a little jokey Jew. We turn jokey into smokey.' Nothing against them personally. Our father who art in heaven used to say they came to our villages, overcharged, undercut. Kept themselves to themselves; wormed in amongst us. You there! Beautiful boy, go to the others. Quick! He smiles. Perhaps he thinks I've come to play with him. He sings to himself; seems indifferent to all our might. The Holy Father also smiles. 'Benediction, my children. War is hell. Do your duty. Judas had his part to play in the mystery; the Jews have been chosen to atone for their sins of rejection of Jesus the Christ. So we beat them; beat them into the transport. I shout. 'Boy! You there! Kneel down. Kneel!' He smiles. I squeeze the trigger. The bullet sings as it floats towards his face. His head explodes, like a watermelon. Hi there! Hi there! Dance with me, Kyrylo! Alexi! You fucking Russian pig. Why are you not dancing? Drink. Drink and dance. Kyrylo! I can see two of you. Terrible things happen in war. Later we work with the *Einsatzgruppen* in Galcia and in the Ukraine, our homeland. Later still we go to Frankfurt am Oder. Guard Battalion 201. In April 1942. Consult the records, my friend. You will see we fought bravely against Soviet partisans. We did our best for Christ and the Holy Father of Rome. I was not yet twenty. No more than a boy, doing my duty. He visits me, over and over again. He's there now. Look! Why are they such a vindictive people? A lifetime has passed. Forgive and forget. (*Sings.*) 'You are my heart's delight and where you are I long to be, you, make my darkness light when like a star you shine on me.' Richard Tauber was a Jew. He was also a gentleman. A decent, clean Jew. How long do they go on wanting revenge? I swear, if I had known what was happening, I would have gone into those camps myself and pulled those Jew boys out of the flames. A man who has worked hard all his life, who has been a relatively good man, who paid his taxes and looked after his family; who lived with his feet firmly on the earth should not be subjected to such bad dreams. I'm fine, my darling Hugo. I see the humour in all things. That great pall of smoke was their last signal, their act of final defiance; the reward of stubborn intransigence. And I must say your grandson is just as beautiful as my darling Lotte; for an Englishman he is most unusual. Hey there! Hey there! Dance with me, Kyrylo. Sebastian! Why are you not dancing? Drink. Drink and dance. Kyrylo! I can see two of you.

HUGO: (*Laughing.*) See three of him. Have another drink.

PETER: That's very kind of you. My granddaughter got married today. I am so proud. She is my joy in this dark and twisted world.

HUGO: And my grandson Simon?

PETER: He is beautiful. Talented. He almost deserves her, Hugo Bauer. Bauer? Bauer? You have a German name.
(*HUGO laughs again.*)
Why do you keep laughing?

HUGO: Peter, my dear friend. Haven't you yet realised? I'm Jewish. I'm a Yid. We're Jewish. Your granddaughter has married a Yid. We've planted our seed inside you, Peter. Would you care for another drink?
(*PETER is transfixed, lost for words. The others still dance in slow motion to the gramophone record. YOUNG ADELE and YOUNG HUGO have also joined in. The music is by Mussorgsky.*)

PETER: This music is called 'Songs and Dances of Death.' The scene. A battlefield. All day the battle has raged, but now the night brings quiet. The moon climbs, appears from behind stark clouds. Death wakes up, looks at me from within your eyes, then surveys the battlefield. Death the Commander in Chief calls upon all the dead to arise for a last roll call. And he's gone. Gone. With all the other dead of the earth. And it is peace at last. Just the silence.
(*The wind howls.*)
My dear fellow. We are both victims of the same war.

(*He holds out his arms to embrace HUGO. They embrace and sway as they hold each other close.*)

Hi there! Hi there! Dance with me, Kyrylo! Alexi! You fucking Russian pig. Why are you not dancing? Drink. Drink and dance. Kyrylo! I can see two of you.

HUGO: Have a nice day.

(*He strangles PETER. The people dance on as PETER lies gurgling on the ground, his tongue poking out of his mouth.*)

MRS WEBER: He's well away.

HUGO: Absolutely.

MRS WEBER: Glad to see you both getting on so well. (*She rejoins the dancing.*)

(*PETER suddenly stands and stiffly walks towards the others, with arms outstretched, like Frankenstein's monster. Then he opens his opens, puts two fingers up to HUGO, laughs mockingly and re-joins the dance.*)

HUGO: (*To SIMON.*) The wedding gift. Please open it now.

(*LOTTE unwraps the parcel to reveal the menorah. MRS BAUER appears.*)

Why do you follow me, Mother? I owe you nothing.

LOTTE: A menorah!

HUGO: The miracle of light. Of life. Despite everything the joy of living. Hold it high. We must still somehow aspire for the mountain top.

(*The people and the scene dissolve. MRS BAUER remains.*)

I am the Knight Commander. And I am pissed. Hugo! Lead the way.

(*He is in the hotel room with YOUNG HUGO and YOUNG ADELE, getting dressed for the award ceremony.*)

How do I look?

YOUNG HUGO: You remind me of a man.

(*HUGO is ready, about to leave the room.*)

MRS BAUER: Haven't you forgotten something?

(*She hands him his violin. He holds the instrument at arm's length.*)

HUGO: Please get lost, Mother. The others now have the decency to stay dead.

MRS BAUER: We must talk.

HUGO: Go back to the others.

MRS BAUER: Others? Goodbye.

YOUNG HUGO: Problems?

HUGO: Problems?

YOUNG HUGO: With the hands?

HUGO: I never have problems with my hands. Let's go.
(*HUGO and YOUNG HUGO are in the street. The HATE BRIGADE have anticipated his journey and encircle him.*)

HATE BRIGADE: Foreigners out! Foreigners out.
Out! Out! Out! Foreigners out! Out! Out! Out!
Heil I.G.Farben! *Heil* Krupps! *Heil* Mercedes Benz!
(*The HATE BRIGADE move on. HUGO confronts YOUNG HUGO.*)

HUGO: Go back to the hotel. Wait for me there.
(*YOUNG HUGO is reluctant but slowly goes. Then an idea occurs to him.*)

YOUNG HUGO: Get me! Get me, you German Nazi bastards! Get me! Get me! You can't get me!
(*The HATE BRIGADE grab him but he laughs as he slips out of their clutches and runs off into the hotel. The HATE BRIGADE angrily pursue, and chase him into the wardrobe. There they are swallowed up. YOUNG HUGO emerges again with YOUNG ADELE. They make a huge tent with bedclothes and chairs. In the street HUGO comes face to face with SIMON.*)

HUGO: Can I play this violin tonight?

SIMON: Can you not play this violin tonight?

HUGO: Give me permission. Tell me I must.

SIMON: I give you permission. Play for all of us.

HUGO: Of course I can do it. Otherwise the sacrifice would all have been in vain. (*He comes forward. He is wearing his medal. He addresses the audience.*) Thank you. I am most moved. I would like to begin with the words of Pastor Niemoeller. A German who stood up against Hitler. 'First they came for the Jews and I did not speak out – because I was not a Jew. Then they came for the Communists and I did not speak out – because I was not a Communist. Then they came for the trade unionists and I did not speak out – because I was not a trade unionist. Then they came for me... and there was no one left to speak out for me.' What happened here? One

madman was enough to poison the acquiescent millions.
But there are some people who hold out hope, who help
us believe that love is stronger than hate, and will
prevail. They inspire and guide us with their courage.
They tell us that we can all yet aspire to be beautiful.
I speak of Pastor Niemoeller and Dietrich Bonhoeffer,
those brave men who went out on a limb to fight against
evil and gave their lives in the process. I include also
those children who were called The White Rose, who
also gave their lives and redeem the rest of us. I did not
want to dwell upon the past, but I seem to have no
choice. The past seems to be the future. Those ugly,
mindless automatons marching in our cities, spewing
obscenities, with their pathetic and cruel acts of violence.
I thought we had all emerged from that nightmare.
Enough of that. Tonight I rid my heart and mind of these
Dark Ages and superimpose the golden light of Schiller's
Ode to Joy. And Goethe. And Holderlin? 'Song, be my
kindly refuge, you, the giver of joy… be tended with
loving care.' So join with me in the prayer of art.
(*Applause.*) I will now play Alban Berg's Violin Concerto.
This is known as 'Night Music'. Our age is night. This
was written in memoriam for the death of Manon
Werfel, daughter of Alma Mahler. I dedicate this final
performance to my sister Klara, whose smile is now but
dust. Hugo! Be with me.
(*YOUNG HUGO has been playing animatedly with YOUNG
ADELE. But somehow and suddenly he has caught HUGO's
plea and he gestures for YOUNG ADELE to be quiet. And
there in the tent he plays (with HUGO) from the second
movement of Berg's concerto. It is perfect and HUGO smiles
across at YOUNG HUGO in the hotel room. Until a crashing
wave of applause engulfs everything. HUGO embraces
SIMON and LOTTE.*)
Remember, Simon, you are Jewish no matter what the
cost. Klara!
(*LOTTE is KLARA as she walks into the wardrobe with
SIMON.*)
Goodbye, Germany.
(*But PETER does one last tipsy little dance.*)

175

PETER: Goodbye, Hugo. Take up your violin. Play. Play. Remember... work makes free.

(*He laughs. The scene fades. Berlin becomes Leeds. HUGO is hurrying through dark streets. A figure lurks in a doorway. It lights up. It is YOUNG HUGO.*)

YOUNG HUGO: 'Where has thou bin since I saw thee? On Ilkley Moor bar tat... Where hast thou bin since I saw thee, where hast thou bin since I saw thee, On Ilkley Moor bar tat – On Ilkley Moor bar tat... On Ilkley Moor bar tat... Then all the worms will eat thee, then all the worms will eat thee, then all the worms will eat thee oop...' Back to Leeds.

HUGO: Yes. To do the concert I couldn't do. I'm late. (*He hurries on.*)

YOUNG HUGO: You're never late for your own funeral. Hey! Wait for me. (*He runs after HUGO.*)

HUGO: I don't need you any more.

YOUNG HUGO: Happy for you.

HUGO: Tell my psyche she can go back to sleep.

YOUNG HUGO: Manage on your own? Good. See you.

HUGO: See you. (*He breathes in.*) Leeds night. Smell the decay. The stench of acquiescence.

(*YOUNG HUGO snaps his fingers. The phalanx of skinhead youth confront HUGO. YOUNG HUGO laughs and disappears.*)

The hate brigade. (*He shouts.*) Hugo! Hugo! Where are you?

HATE BRIGADE: *Sieg heil! Sieg heil!* Keep Britain white! Out with the niggers! Out with the Yids! Out with the Pakis! *Sieg heil! Sieg heil! Sieg heil!* Out with the Yids!

HUGO: So what's new?

BOY: (*From the HATE BRIGADE. Comes close to inspect him.*) What have we here? Jew boy! Jew boy! Jew boy! (*The others take up the cry.*) What's this? (*Grabbing the violin.*) A fiddle. A yiddle mit a fiddle. What is a Jew boy doing in Leeds?

HUGO: I'm doing a concert! I owe them one.

BOY: He owes them one. He's doing a concert. Jew boy! (*All the others laugh. The mood is ugly, menacing, atavistic.*) Do the concert here.

(*The HATE BRIGADE marches around him, chanting.*)

HATE BRIGADE: Jew boy. Jew boy. Jew boy. Jew boy. Jew boy. Get the rich Jew boy! Play! Or we'll do ya!

HUGO: (*Plays a schmaltzy version of 'Yesterday'.*) 'Yesterday, all my troubles seemed so far away. Dadaddadededadade, For I believe in yesterday.' (*They stand around him, loving it, applauding.*)

HATE BRIGADE: Jew boy. Jew boy. Jew boy. Jew boy. Jew boy. Jew boy.

GIRL: (*From the HATE BRIGADE. Speaks out.*) Shut up. Let him play. Listen to him.

HUGO: Thank you. (*Plays a few bars of 'Lark Ascending'.*) Listen! Can I get through to you? Where are you? Where's your brain? Your heart? Let me get through to you. I'm Hugo Bauer. A survivor. I'm famous. The world has heard of me. I want to understand you. We're all the same; all part of the human family.

HATE BRIGADE: You're nothing. You're a Yid. You're dead.

GIRL: Smash his fucking violin. He's a rich, fucking Yid. Piss on him.

HATE BRIGADE: Yid. Yid. Yid. Yid. Yiddle with his fiddle.
(*They try to grab the violin. HUGO struggles to keep it.*)
You Yids control the world.

HUGO: I can't even control my mind.
(*The encircling mob whip off their masks. They are his family, the LEVYS, ADELE, SIMON, all the people he has met since he first entered the bedroom.*)
Now even my ghosts are anti-Semites.

HATE BRIGADE: (*Whispering, almost silent as they goad him.*) Hugo! The Jew boy! The chosen. The Yid. Jew boy! Hugo, the Jew boy. The chosen. The Yid. Hugo. The Jew boy. The Jew boy. The Jew boy.

HUGO: Hugo!
(*He cowers as YOUNG HUGO appears. The HATE BRIGADE march around and around then disperse. HUGO is now ragged, unkempt.*)

YOUNG HUGO: The concert.

HUGO: Yes, now. It's late. (*Hugging his violin like a lover.*) They didn't break you. My very old and perfect signorina. I am a double Jew. If I could smash this violin. Which way is home? Home. Joke. Seven wealthy towns compete for Homer dead, where the living Homer begged his bread.

YOUNG HUGO: We must clean you up. Keep up appearances.

HUGO: My dear, young friend. Let me lean on you. My childhood. You stayed with me though you knew me. You knew I was nothing. A fraud, a coward. A hypocrite. A liar.

YOUNG HUGO: Who gave you permission to be a liar?

HUGO: God. He talked to me last night.

YOUNG HUGO: Liar.

HUGO: Would God talk to a liar? Get me back to my hotel. (*YOUNG HUGO helps him back to his feet. HUGO seems broken as he leans heavily on YOUNG HUGO. They re-enter the hotel room.*)

Hugo, I want my mother. I never said goodbye to my mother. Where's my mother?

YOUNG HUGO: *Voila*! (*He goes to YOUNG ADELE in the improvised tent.*)

MRS BAUER: (*Coming out of the wardrobe.*) Hugo!

HUGO: I wanted to see you. To say I'm finished with you.

MRS BAUER: I understand.

HUGO: She understands! You died once. I died all your deaths, over and over again.

MRS BAUER: You had the gift.

HUGO: You gave me a living death.

MRS BAUER: You lived for all of us.

HUGO: I wanted to die with you.

MRS BAUER: A mother can't win. Everyone blames the mother. I did what I thought was best.

HUGO: You let me go.

MRS BAUER: Because I loved you.

HUGO: And I've hated you all my life. Because you were the one person I ever loved. I was the sacrifice.

MRS BAUER: Can a dead mother apologise?

HUGO: No! I'm finished with you.

MRS BAUER: Hugo!

HUGO: Go to hell.

MRS BAUER: I'm there already. It's where all the innocent
are. (*Turns, about to go.*)

HUGO: Yours was the greater crime. Mother, hold me.
(*She holds him. They hug and sway together.*)
Is it too late for an old man to grow up?

MRS BAUER: The dead are not very good with advice.

HUGO: And now you must go. Go forever.

MRS BAUER: Yes.

HUGO: Good. Goodbye.

MRS BAUER: Goodbye. (*Goes.*)

HUGO: Mother! Mother! (*Falls onto the bed and cries.*)
I'll never see her again. Never. Never.
(*YOUNG HUGO and YOUNG ADELE giggle inside
the tent.*)
Stand up. Get on with it. You are now a Knight
Commander! All fear has left you. You are in command
of the night. Where is it? I've lost my German medal.
(*YOUNG HUGO and YOUNG ADELE appear from the
tent. They have obviously just been naughty.*)

YOUNG HUGO: We've done it.

YOUNG ADELE: We've done it.

YOUNG HUGO: Did you enjoy it?

YOUNG ADELE: Not sure. It could have been very nice.
Thank you.

YOUNG HUGO: No, thank you.

YOUNG ADELE: (*Yawns.*) I'm tired. I'm going home.

YOUNG HUGO: Where's home?

YOUNG ADELE: (*Shrugs.*) See you. (*Enters the wardrobe and
leaves the door open.*)

YOUNG HUGO: See you.

HUGO: Hugo! In. (*Holds the door open for YOUNG HUGO.*)

YOUNG HUGO: Wait! (*Handing HUGO the telephone.
HUGO doesn't understand.*) You're doing a concert,
remember. Tell them you'll be a little late.

HUGO: (*Taking a swig of whisky.*) Hand me that thing.
(*YOUNG HUGO hands him the violin and takes up his
own.*)

Who's afraid? (*Like Churchill.*) We have nothing to fear except fear itself. Listen! (*He plays from 'Lark Ascending'.*) I can do it. When a bird soars, it soars. It ascends. What does it care if yesterday its babies were eaten by an eagle? It has no memory. I can do it. I'll do it. There are many ways to get over a wall. Phone!

(*YOUNG HUGO complies, hands him the telephone. HUGO dials then assumes an Irish voice.*)

Is that the police?... Listen carefully. This is a coded message. This is a coded message. Cast a cold eye, on life, on death. Horseman ride by. I repeat. Cast a cold eye on life, on death, horseman ride by. There will be a bomb in the Leeds concert hall this evening. It is timed to explode at exactly eight thirty-seven. Thank you.

(*Puts the phone down. They both laugh at his audacity.*)

YOUNG HUGO: Coward.

HUGO: Yes. Human. Unfortunately. I'll play when I choose. I'll play for me. I'm resting. Licking my wounds. Enjoying my distance. Not playing for them, any more.

YOUNG HUGO: Like hell.

HUGO: Maybe one day. And I will endure. Survivors have no choice. Retreat is not such a dirty word. Maybe I'll find a new courage when I approach the foothills of middle age.

YOUNG HUGO: (*Laughs.*) Hugo! You're old! Haven't you looked in the mirror recently? It's you for deep, dark endlessness, quite soon.

HUGO: You see Hugo, there's no end to crisis. Don't even try to solve your crisis because another one will surely take its place, and it's bound to be much worse. Life is crisis. Learn to love your crisis.

(*A knock on the door. YOUNG HUGO opens it. ADELE enters.*)

How is...

ADELE: Don't speak. Don't say anything.

(*HUGO holds out his arms. She goes to him and they clutch together, swaying.*)

I feel nothing. Nothing.

HUGO: The dead demand too much.

ADELE: I feel nothing. Nothing. Hold me. Tight. Hard. Harder.

(*HUGO complies, they still sway together.*)

HUGO: What can I say?

ADELE: Say nothing.

HUGO: He suffered? He's better off now?

ADELE: Homilies.

HUGO: You're free?

ADELE: Free? (*She laughs.*)

HUGO: He was a long time dying. I'm sorry.

ADELE: Love is honed by a lifetime of need and use. He's dead. I'll get used to it

HUGO: May I make love to you?

ADELE: No.

HUGO: Why did you come?

ADELE: I needed to tell you.

HUGO: Thank you. We're both free now.

ADELE: Yes. I must go. You understand.

HUGO: Yes. Good luck.

ADELE: We'll be in touch.

HUGO: One last thing. Will you marry me?

ADELE: No.

HUGO: I see. Goodbye.

ADELE: Goodbye. (*She goes.*)

YOUNG HUGO: Here! Catch! (*Not a smile but the violin.*)

HUGO: At least I know who I am. I make music.

YOUNG HUGO: Not tonight you're not, mate.

HUGO: If I am not a violinist what am I? A man holds on to his profession. It gives him identity. Retirement is death. Go amongst strangers. It is almost the first question they ask. What do you do for a living? Actually I am an abortionist. Really? How interesting. No, seriously, I work in an abattoir. Oh? Really? How... interesting. Actually I shoot rats in the tube tunnels at night. Really? How interesting. I am a violinist. A violinist. This violin is an extension of myself. It is me. I am it. It has grown into my flesh. It has become an extension of my hands. In the caves each of us took on

the job he was most suited for. I am a violinist. Watch
their eyes light up, Hugo. Listen to the way they listen.
See how they are lifted. The whole audience rise up into
the air, as one, applauding. They bounce off the ceiling.
The mystical marriage. I enter them. They enter me.
Timelessness. Here I cheat death and it is the closest
they get to God. My mortal audience. I give them
dreams. I spin them otherness. Music sings of dreams
and purpose. Man reaching out; seeking immortality.
I fool them that there is a purpose to all this. Doesn't
that redeem me?

YOUNG HUGO: Fuck redemption.

HUGO: How dare you! How dare you swear!

YOUNG HUGO: Hugo, play. It's the only thing you do well.

HUGO: If he dares to resurrect himself again I'll kick him
in the balls.

YOUNG HUGO: Who? Hitler?

HUGO: No, God! (*Laughs.*) We have a special relationship.
I leave him alone. He leaves me alone. Hugo, no one will
call with the answer. There's only us. Us alone. Please
don't let me get God. Please! Promise? Alzheimers?
Maybe. God? Never. I'm relying on you. Anyway God,
I believe, is somewhere else, currently working on a less
ambitious project.
(*They both play from Bach's double violin concerto for a few
minutes.*)
Hugo.

YOUNG HUGO: Yes, Hugo?

HUGO: It's goodbye, for now.

YOUNG HUGO: I see. You remind me of a man.

HUGO: What man?

YOUNG HUGO: The man with the power?

HUGO: What power?

YOUNG HUGO: The power of the hoodoo. (*Enters the
wardrobe.*)

HUGO: Who do?

YOUNG HUGO: You do.

HUGO: I do what?

YOUNG HUGO: You remind me of a man. Bye.

HUGO: At least leave me a smile.

YOUNG HUGO: You're taking my last one.

(*He smiles bravely then wipes it across HUGO's face. HUGO closes the wardrobe door. All is silent. But we hear his voice trailing off into the distance, becoming more and more babylike and pathetic as it echoes in endlessness.*)

I want my mother. I want my mother. I want my mother. I'm afraid of the dark… I want my mummy… I want my mummy… I want my mummy…

(*His pathetic child's voice trails off into endlessness. HUGO now has the mask of the smile firmly fixed to his face. It is night. The room is almost in darkness. The telephone rings. HUGO ignores it. It stops ringing.*)

HUGO: I am Hugo. I am. I am The Knight Commander!

(*He laughs terribly, deep and sardonically, then he puts the violin to his ear.*) And the songs. The sorrows. The dreams. The prayers. The cries. The laughter. All my faces, all my ghosts call in the night.

(*The telephone rings, but again he ignores it. He takes up his violin to play, but at first he can make no sound. He is poised in space. Then in the far distance, from the deep universe within the wardrobe comes the distinct sweet sound of Vaughan Williams' 'Lark Ascending'. HUGO plays serenely, his eyes closed, transported by his music.*)

The End.

Also published by Oberon Books:

Shalom Bomb: Scenes From My Life

'Not since Coleridge's opium addiction has there been
such a seismic account of a journey into hell and back...
and there are jokes.'

Michael Kustow

'A white-knuckle ride through his life with Kops at your
shoulder – always disarmingly honest, infuriating, suicidally
optimistic and a brilliant companion.'

Joanna Lumley

ISBN: 1 84002 112 8   Price: £15.99

Kops: Plays One

'*The Hamlet of Stepney Green* is a hymn of
confident affirmation.'

Colin MacInnes, *Encounter*

'This beautifully written tragi-comedy.'

Sunday Independent on *Playing Sinatra*

'No other living playwright matches Kops in the
virtuoso handling of dream logic.'

Observer on *Ezra*

ISBN: 1 84002 071 7   Price: £9.99